Don't CURSE Your CRISIS

Dr. Angela L. Corprew Boyd
& 15 Empowered Co-Authors
Propelled To VICTORY

Don't CURSE Your CRISIS by Dr. Angela L. Corprew Boyd

Published by Bell-Boyd Publishing

P.O. Box 15142

Chesapeake, VA 23328

www.angieboydministries.org

womenempowered98@aol.com

Unless otherwise noted, all Scripture quotations are from the King James Version of the Bible.

Scripture quotations are taken from *The Holy Bible,* New Living Translation, copyright © 2004, 2015, by Tyndale House Foundation. Used by permission of Tyndale House Publishers, Carol Stream, IL 60188. All rights reserved.

Scripture quotations marked NKJV are from *The Holy Bible*, New King James Version, copyright © 2020 by permission of Tyndale House Foundation. Used by permission of Tyndale House Publishers, Carol Stream, IL 60188. All rights reserved.

Scripture quotations marked CSB are from the Christian Standard Bible, copyright © 2017. Used by permission of B & H Publishers Group, Nashville, TN 37234. All rights reserved.

ISBN: 978-0-9800536-2-3

Dedication

This book is dedicated to every individual, whether ally or enemy, who played a role in our elevation. We did not curse our crises, but they empowered us. Thank you!

Acknowledgment

Thank you, God, for allowing me to be the Visionary Author of this collaboration and empowering the co-authors to share the crises in their lives. We thank God for every experience that shaped and molded us in the development of our manuscripts. God was pulling out of us the narratives that would escort us to our blessings amid the crises.

CONTENTS

Forward

As an ordained minister in Birmingham, Alabama, I have witnessed the destruction that traumatic events have on individuals and the collateral damage that impacts families. Counseling individuals who have dealt with crises and life-altering events is difficult to comprehend and even overcome. Whether dealing with sexual assault, the death of a close loved one, abuse, drugs, depression or even violence, life takes on a different meaning. Getting to a place of sharing is a milestone and a vital part of the healing process.

As tumultuous as life can sometimes get, it is important to see life on a different avenue. The perspective you choose may dictate what road your life travels.

This book gives a personal approach, from different perspectives, when a crisis in your life suddenly lands at your feet. The authors tell different but unique events of how life affected their journey and show how God navigates each soul to a place of calm, peace, and empowerment.

Satan has a plan with a purpose to keep you looking back. We quickly sink into a dark place with a focus on our assaults, failures, sins, and mistakes. If we remain in our hurt, we stay stuck in our past. This collaboration is a guide to achievement, enlightenment, and a class of wholeness.

Each survivor speaks to you from a prism of pain. Despite years of inadequacy wrapped in emotional neglect and unworthiness, healing takes shape. Each author displays the ability to convey pain and trauma and usher in a source of strength and love through the power of God.

Patrick L. Henry

Crisis Camouflaged

by **Dr. Angela L. Corprew Boyd**

Crisis

It clouds my mind

I don't have good judgment

It can't be renewed

My mind is confused

Crisis

It's a heavy load on my feet

It burdens my heart

It smothers my soul

It's dead weight

Crisis

It's life!

Part of my journey!

Part of my purpose!

Part of my becoming!

Crisis

Troubles

Trials

Tribulations

From dishonor to honor

From disgrace to grace

From appalling to appealing

From shame to success

From failure to fortune

Accept it

Embrace it

Enjoy the VICTORY in it!

CRISIS, it's part of life!

Don't CURSE Your CRISIS

Mother, international preacher, leadership consultant, certified life coach, author, mentor, and founder of Women Empowered in the Millennium, Inc. and The Empowerment Circle, Dr. Angela Corprew Boyd, affectionately known as Dr. Angie, is a change agent who empowers others to fulfill their destinies. Amazon Best Selling Author, she has three books, *If I Perish, Let Me Perish, But I'm Next, Church Hurt: The Wounded Trying to Heal and Removing the Fear,* a collaboration with eleven co-authors on their journey from fear to freedom. She was recently recognized as Mentor of the Year in Virginia by ACHI Magazine. Founder and host of the *Empowerment with Dr. Angie* talk show, she celebrates women's work and motivates viewers by sharing words of empowerment. Dr. Corprew Boyd earned her Doctorate in Strategic Leadership from Regent University and served in Chesapeake Public Schools for over 30 years as a teacher, assistant principal, and human resources administrator. She has also worked as an academic vice-principal in the United Arab Emirates and served in leadership with Cornerstone International Church. She immensely loves parenting three adult children, Devin, Donovan, and Dawn, and three grandchildren, Noah, Timberlynn, and Wynter.

Connect with Dr. Angie at www.angieboydministries.org

CRISIS 1

The Pain of "NO" from My Crisis

Dr. Angela L. Corprew Boyd

—☀—☀—☀—☀—☀—☀—☀—

❝No! Not this time; we selected someone else!" "You're a great leader; however, someone else is better for this position." "No, you need a little more experience." "We were thinking about you but went in a different direction." "Dr. Boyd, if you had more experience in leading, maybe next year you will be considered." "Yes, you were considered, but we decided to go with someone more experienced." "You do not qualify for that school." "Give us a few more years, and we will see if a principalship is available." "We think you need to be more developed." Every time I interviewed for a principalship, I heard those rejecting words from upper management in the twenty-two years of waiting. After hearing them for years, I began questioning my leadership, experience, and self-worth. "How many times does "NO" have to slap you in the face before you feel rejected, despondent, and devalued as a person and leader?" This became the norm for my professional career. I summed up every depressing "NO" as a curse that couldn't be broken or redirected. One day, I finally decided to stop camouflaging what I was enduring and called one of my mentors. I asked my mentor, "So, when will this crisis of rejection for promotion end?" She responded, "It will end when you stop seeking man for promotion and start seeking God." I hung up the phone, fell to my knees, and began to sob uncontrollably.

I had heard every cliché from family, friends, colleagues, and mentors. "It is going to happen. You will be promoted. It will not be long now. It is going to happen suddenly." It was promising to hear those words, but it did not take the pain of rejection away when I heard, "Not now." It still means "NO!" In my mind, the thought of "NO" became exasperated. It spread like poison to every area of my life, contaminating every affirmation I spoke. I was crippled and saw no movement forward in my present state, but I would not allow them to stop me. I was not going to let this crisis deter me. Those "NOS" pushed me to manage the situation myself; I sought promotion on my own. What a disaster!

I complicated my crisis by taking matters into my own hands. I became impatient and began to share my denial stories with those I thought I could trust. Instead of my colleagues, whom I had considered trustworthy, giving me wisdom and advice of being patient, they agreed that upper management was doing me wrong. They agreed that I should have been promoted to principalship by now. They agreed that it was the "good old boy" system and being a Black female with a doctorate was a threat, and I should go to another system where I would be appreciated. I thought this was great advice, so I did. I prepared my resume and received the most exceptional references from leadership within the school district and those who knew me personally outside of it. I made phone calls, sent emails, and delivered resumes to surrounding school districts. Amazingly, I received a phone call from another school district's assistant superintendent to extend a meeting to me. Overwhelmed with excitement, I scheduled the appointment. When the day came, I was ready to move on and say my goodbyes to my present employer because I knew I would be leaving his office with an offer in administration. If I could tell everyone else to "speak and expect," I knew this affirmation would also work in my favor.

When I entered the assistant superintendent's office, he invited me to sit at the table. He said, "I was very impressed with your credentials." I smiled and said, "Thank you." He asked, "May I share a 'word' with you?" I paused and thought, "a word." The phrase caught me by surprise, but I looked at him and said, "Sure." His word was, "The crisis you're in right now is the working of God." You can imagine my discomfort at the time. My eyes bulged and became misty, and my body went numb. I was in shock. My facial expression was a dead giveaway that allowed him to permit me to speak. I first said, "I am tired of being rejected, and I do not see the reason for constantly being refused a promotion. I have consulted with my colleagues, and they encouraged me to pursue my options." He repeated,

"The crisis you're in right now is the working of God." While sitting there, I had a transparent moment; I did not want to hear what God had to say, but He revealed that I was so focused on the reason and not the revelation of the crisis. God used that meeting as a setup to ensure that I put myself back in a position for His plan, not mine. Sitting in that office at the table, I began to analyze why none of my colleagues told me how immature I was behaving and that I was acting unprofessional. I was acting as if someone owed me something because of my credentials. Honestly, I felt I had given, served, and my record spoke for itself. "Why shouldn't I want to be promoted?" But that was not the problem. The problem was I never sought God to resolve my crisis. I sought people. BAD DECISION! Before our meeting ended, the assistant superintendent challenged me with two questions: "What lesson should you learn in this crisis?" When they say "NO," what are you learning?"

I left the office and sat in my car in the parking lot and began to process the questions, "What should you have learned from their NOS?" What came to mind, I was concentrating on the reason and not the revelation. Indeed, God was telling me something but my attitude, dislike for the pressure and pain from the process, and the constant resounding "NO" wouldn't allow me to see what I needed to learn. I drove from that parking lot and had a little talk with Jesus. The thirty minutes from that office to my home seemed like an eternity. God used that time to soften my heart because I had closed it off to Him. I willingly surrendered so that God could speak to me. By that time, I was sobbing uncontrollably, again, when I reached my destination. I was sitting in my home's driveway; the fact that God loved me so much that He would orchestrate a simple meeting to tell me what I needed to do blew my mind. It was an epiphany when I came to myself, like the Prodigal Son (Luke 15:11-32). God revealed that I had been camouflaging the crisis, and I did not learn the lessons He was teaching me.

He quickly brought to my remembrance a book that I had been recently reading by Maya Angelou; I *Know Why the Caged Bird Sings*. I recalled a quote that pierced my inner man and awakened the wisdom in me. She said, "If life teaches us anything, it may be that it is necessary to suffer disappointments. Look at a diamond; It is the result of extreme pressure. Less pressure, it is just a crystal; less than that, it is just coal; and less than that, it is just plain dirt." I could now answer the question, "What should you have learned?" All the pain from "NO" should have taught me lessons from the pressure of my crisis. Perseverance, patience, and purpose should have pushed me to understand the revelation of their "NOS" and my crisis.

Perseverance is persistence in doing something despite difficulty or delay in achieving success. It means being hardworking and finishing what was started, despite barriers and obstacles. This was a struggle for me because I was still focusing on the negativity of the crisis. If God would remove the pressures, the pain, and the rejection from their "NOS," I could have persevered, but that would be a contradiction of the definition. There was a time I was close to wavering in my faith, but that would mean giving in to "NO." Not so! I decided I would not be moved again because someone did not see or respect my God given gifts, talents, or education I worked diligently to attain. I had to stand in what God promised me, promotion. What escorted me through this crisis was God's word. "Blessed is a man who perseveres under trial; for once he has been approved, he will receive the crown of life which the Lord has promised to those who love Him," (James 1:2). Perseverance led my patience to be tested.

Patience is accepting or tolerating problems or suffering without becoming annoyed or anxious. It was not easy! When everyone around me was promoted, I would ask myself, "What do they have that I don't." Comparing myself with others did not help in my crisis. It hurt me. I began to question my faith in God's word. First, the Bible says, "God will give you the desires of your heart," (Psalms 37:4). Secondly, "God will withhold no good thing from you," (Psalms 84:11). Thirdly, "Promotion comes from God," (Psalms 75:6-7). I knew all this was true, but when does the manifestation of the word come? I was qualified. I was experienced. I was equipped, and from a Christian perspective, I was highly favored, but none of it seemed to matter. The challenge was being patient with an attitude of thanksgiving, hoping God would honor His word. I had to have faith in

Psalms, 37:7, "Rest in the Lord, and wait patiently for Him: fret not thyself because of him who prospereth in His way, because of the man who bringeth wicked devices to pass." Patience was connected to my purpose.

Purpose is the reason something is done, created, or exists. I deeply pondered this crisis and asked God, "Are you in this?" His response through scripture is, "And we know that all things work together for good to them that love God, to them who are the called according to his purpose," (Romans 8:28). That was another WOW moment for me. Is all this suffering necessary for my next level? It was because God was equipping me for something more remarkable than a principalship, but it was His purpose that I did not see. I wanted something for myself, but I learned, "Many are the plans in a man's heart, but it is the Lord's purpose that prevails" (Proverbs 19:21). So, I settled with God's decision, Him placing me where my presence needed to be.

A few months later, when I was no longer having an internal fight within myself or an external struggle with the "system," I saw the manifestation of perseverance, patience, and purpose begin to pay off. God continued to order my steps and execute His plan for my life, but because the crisis had settled in me and debilitated my sense of understanding, I could not see what God was doing. I, again, was about to curse the blessing He had waiting for me. Another visit from an angel within the system offered me an opportunity to serve as an assistant principal at a high school. It was a promotion but not a principalship. My thoughts were, "Here we go again." I could hear the whisper of "NO" in my ear, and because of it, I was about to mess up God's plan. When the offer was extended, I was resistant and stubborn, and said, "I don't think so." The look in the visitor's eyes was shocking. He then asked me to think about it and let him know in a few days. I deliberated over the weekend and concluded that since they said "NO," I would give them a "NO." But we know God, when we are about to mess up His plan, He sends that angel again to help us to know it is Him.

My daughter, Dawn, knew of my desire to become a principal. We also discussed early on if I had interviewed for the upcoming year. She randomly asked during the weekend of my deliberation if I had heard anything about my promotion. In a sigh of disappointment, I said, "No." I jokingly said, "Maybe they will assign me to your high school, and I can serve there." The reaction of jubilation was not expected. She barreled into me and said, "Oh my God, that would be awesome." I did not know how to respond to her response. You see, it was her school that the assistant superintendent had asked me to consider. I knew when he told me the school, I would say no, but after seeing my daughter's reaction when I suggested it could be a possibility, I began to consider it. God certainly has a way of making sure His plan is executed. I was still unsure about accepting this new assignment; however, I planned a meeting with the high school principal.

Despite my feelings of uncertainty, I met with the principal. We had a great relationship from serving together a few years prior to this offer. We chatted for a while, and she said something that confirmed that I was to accept, "We need your presence in this building." I was still allowing feelings of disappointment and pain from the never-ending crisis to overwhelm me. Although it was confirmed twice, my flesh tried to choose for me, but I released the stronghold and accepted the offer. An overwhelming peace enveloped me, and I sensed this crisis was ending; however, I was not out of it yet. I took a pivot, not knowing what God was about to do, but the revelation was about to be unveiled.

The new school year began months later, and I was a part of one of the best administrative teams in the school district. I was at peace, and my presence in the building was needed. I wholeheartedly served the teachers, parents, and students. This was one of the best years of my professional career, and I almost cursed what God was trying to bless me with. This assignment was precisely what I needed. The pain and suffering were not more significant than the purpose, but God honored me for staying in it until I saw the revelation and stopped focusing on the reason. One day I was sitting in my office, and my principal came in abruptly but excitedly. She stood there peering into my eyes and said, "I'm going to let you graduate, Dawn." She then turned around and left as abruptly as she came into the office. I gathered my thoughts and repeated in my mind what she stated. When it finally hit me, what she said, I began to weep. I immediately asked God a series of questions. "Was this crisis about me conferring my daughter's high school diploma upon her? Was this pain and suffering I endured for one of the most significant assignments I could complete as a mom and administrator? Is this why my presence was needed at this high school? Was this crisis for me to fulfill a purpose that You preordained before the foundation of the world, even before Dawn was formed in my womb?" God did respond, "Yes, every time they said 'NO,' my plan for you was being executed for a greater purpose." And to think, I almost cursed what brought me to this place of favor and VICTORY! Since retiring, I continue to work for this school district, and I am forever grateful that my crisis has blessed others.

> **My crisis EMPOWERED me to**
> **experience God's promised plan.**

A re you in a crisis? If so, do not curse it by asking God to prematurely take you out of it. There is no lesson learned when you give in to the pain of rejection, disappointment, divorce, abandonment, and doubt from your crisis. God is in your crisis because He is the creator of your plan and knows there is suffering attached to your journey. Jeremiah 29:11, "For I know the plans I have for you, declares the Lord, plans to prosper you and not to harm you, plans to give you hope and a future." Many of you have found yourselves orchestrating your plan, and because it has failed, it clouds what God wants to do with and for you in your crisis. Release your choice to operate your plan. Yes, you will go through a crisis, problem, affliction, shame, embarrassment, and suffering, but know God is in it. Romans 8:18, "For I reckon that the sufferings of this present time are not worthy to be compared with the glory which shall be revealed in us." In the narratives to follow, you will discover not to curse your crisis but walk in the VICTORY that evolves from it, and you will be EMPOWERED!

Dr. Patricia J. Williams is a mother of three, grandmother of four, motivational speaker, international evangelist, and certified personal and executive coach. She received her Bachelor's in Psychology from Old Dominion University, Master of Arts and Educational Specialist degrees from Regent University, and Doctorates from Regent University and Newburg Theological Seminary. She is a living testimony that you can begin again, finishing her bachelor's at fifty-two and her doctorate at sixty-five. She is currently employed as an Instructional Compliance Coordinator with Richmond Public Schools. She is also the founder of Abundant Living, a network of resources for people through coaching, mentoring, workshops, conferences, and retreats. Most of all, she is a servant whose passion is to help others experience the abundant life God desires for them. As she often tells her audiences, "You are never too old, never too young, or never too anything, if you are willing to leave the land of "familiar" and start again."

Connect with Dr. Williams at drpatwms@gmail.com

CRISIS 2

When Pain Heals

Dr. Patricia Williams

—☓—☓—☓—☓—☓—☓—☓—

The rain was beating hard on the windshield of my car. I could hear the brushing of my windshield wipers sweeping the rain across the windshield. I meant to get new wipers weeks prior but never took the time. I hated driving in the rain, and I hated driving at night. I hated doing what I had to do that night in the rain. I never thought I would be leaving—leaving my marriage, my preschool with forty-nine students and nine teachers, and my position as co-pastor of a well-known ministry. I was in a crisis that was not going to go away any time soon.

It was not just raining outside. The rain was beating down inside my heart as I drove away from everything that had been so familiar to me for so long. It seemed as if I would lose my breath or lose my mind at any moment. This choice would rock my world like a rocket blasting out of the atmosphere, leaving behind dust so thick that anyone in its path would be covered with it. Leaving landed me in a turbulent emotional place where I questioned whether I could survive on my own.

What made me think I could choose on my own—a choice for me and my sanity?

My life was luxurious. I lived in a 3,500-square-foot home with four bedrooms, three full baths, and a swimming pool. My husband and I drove luxury cars. We traveled around the world on the dream vacation of a lifetime, cruising through the islands of Tahiti. But every day was ruled by my silence, my willingness to say only those words that were measured and weighed so as not to trigger the usual response, "Don't make me mad, Pat!" I knew he would never hit me again because I finally had him arrested, and he stayed in jail for three days. One day, I was tired of being told, "That doesn't look good on you. It is raining. You do not wear white in the rain. Put on something else. Don't you know how to dress yet?" That day, I dared to use my voice. I was so used to walking on eggshells, but not this time.

"Why do you care so much about how I dress and what I wear every Sunday? You did not care when we dated for fifteen years," I said. The response was raw but explicit. "You were my whore. Now you are my wife."

I have never been punched in the stomach with full force or had the wind knocked out of me. I was sitting in the chair across from the man I had been with for over thirty-three years— the man I had sacrificed so much for in many ways and the man I loved. I missed many of my children's life celebrations because they hated how he physically abused me and could not understand why I stayed. I missed my parents' 50th wedding anniversary celebration because he wanted me to go to another church with him. Birthdays, anniversaries, and funerals of loved ones—all missed because I allowed him to isolate me. I sat there stunned and in disbelief. Then I heard the still, quiet voice that I knew so well. "That is enough. You can leave. I will handle him." Finally, I got up and walked out of the room. It was over. Or was it?

Was God telling me I could leave? Was I free? It was not as if I had not left multiple times before, but I always went back. Whenever I sought counseling from someone in the church, it was always the same. "Baby, maybe God wants to use you to deliver him." "Stick it out. Better to have somebody than to be alone." But I had somebody, and I was still alone.

This time would be different. I was tired, and I was sick. Over the years, my body screamed at me in so many ways. Hypertension, anxiety attacks, diabetes, glaucoma, and finally, severe sleep apnea were all signs that the stress of walking on eggshells had taken its toll. My body was in a state of "dis ease." It would be easy to place all the blame on him and say it was all his fault. My crisis was not about my husband. It was about facing my mistakes and confronting the fear that had driven my life for so long. The more I exposed myself to people and learned about life through the Bible and education, the more I realized I had given up my control to fear. Now it was time for fear to take a backseat. I was ready to drive my car, make my own choices, and face every fear that had held me hostage for so long.

After two years filled with sporadic marriage counseling appointments that seemed to focus on my husband's anger and his need to control me, it became clear that the marriage was over. My husband did not want things to be better. He just wanted me to come back, and I had moved far away from the land of "familiar." There was no going back. Before I could move forward, I had to reflect on "familiar." The years between high school and my first marriage were filled with abusive relationships, depression, suicide attempts, and anger. I was angry with God and angry with myself.

The God in the Bible and the God in my life were not the same. Church folk kept telling me to straighten up. Some said, "You'll never outlive your mistakes." Some said, "You'll never be the same." But I did not want to be the same. I knew about other young ladies in the church who got pregnant out of wedlock. But things were hush-hush, and then there was a wedding shower, and they got married. I knew the preacher that got drunk on the weekend and preached in the pulpit on Sunday morning. I saw the pianist with the black eye underneath the sunglasses playing for the choir on Sunday morning. It was like it was normal. No one talked about it, even if you asked. In my mind, it was okay because it happened to church folks. I never saw my father abuse my mother, but no one bothered to explain that this was not normal or godly. It seemed okay to be disrespected, to live a double life, and to allow yourself to be abused in every feasible way. It was all a part of the "weeping may endure for a night, but joy cometh in the morning" syndrome.

I still had to make sense of the choices I made. If I did not, I was doomed to repeat the story, and I wanted this chapter of my story to have a different ending. The first two weeks after I left the marriage, I stayed in a friend's home in a gated community so far back in the woods that I did not have phone reception until I drove to the corner of the road. It was a beautiful home on the lake with a golf course on the other side. I watched as the golfers stroked the ball across the course. My life had been like that little golf ball. I had allowed someone else to bounce me around. Now I was the one with the golf club, and I could hit that ball anywhere I pleased. I refused to talk to anyone except a few trusted friends. My phone was filled with messages pleading with me to have mercy. Come back. Suck it up. Stop being selfish. I chose not to respond and deleted the messages. I was no longer a people-pleaser. I was a God-pleaser, and I could sense God was in control.

After visiting my parents for two weeks, I returned to spend time with my daughter and map out the rest of my life.

Early morning walks became a classroom for my personal growth. As I learned about myself, I faced the reality that I did not like myself very much. I was filled with shame, guilt, disappointment, and fear. I was starting over at sixty-five years old. Would anyone hire me? I was supposed to be retiring, not starting a new job. During one of those walks, I became familiar with Lisa Nichols and her story. I started repeating these three sentences seven times every morning. "Pat, I love you. Pat, I forgive you. Pat, you are good enough." During the first few months, I would only say the sentences on my early morning walks where I could hide the tears underneath my cap. Very few people in my life had told me repeatedly that they loved me. Hearing the words from my mouth pulled at my heartstrings. One day several months later, I stood in front of the mirror in my apartment as I prepared to go to work and said, "Pat, I love you. Pat, I forgive you. Pat, you are good enough." There were no tears, only a big smile, and glistening eyes. I believed in myself. I liked myself—no, I loved myself. It was not an arrogant love but a love that looked past my mistakes and failures and acknowledged my successes and any and everything in between. I liked living with myself, and I was good enough. At work, I found a new sense of respect. I was like a baby with a big round lollipop. People appreciated my wisdom and experience, including my white hair.

In March 2020, I called my husband. I sensed in my spirit that something was not right. We never completely stopped communicating. There was a phone call here and there and a letter now and then. Despite everything, I loved him. But I was not going back to the land of "familiar." He had lost his brother a few months earlier, and I knew it had been a painful blow for him. When he answered the phone, his speech sounded slurred, but he was adamant that he had not had a stroke. I wanted to take him to the hospital since I knew he would not go alone. He refused but asked me to attend his doctor's appointment the following week. When I got to the house, I could not believe my eyes. His stomach looked like he was nine months pregnant. He could not walk on his own. I knew he would have to be admitted to the hospital, so I returned to Richmond to get a few clothes and personal items and returned. When I got back two days later, he was even worse. From the doctor's office, they immediately sent us to the emergency room. Moments before he was to go to his room, everything went on lockdown because of COVID-19, and they refused to let me stay with him. He refused to stay without me. We went home.

I lay in bed that night. I knew he was dying and that no one else was willing to take care of him. The same man who had brought so much pain into my life now had no one else to take care of him but me if I was willing. It was the most challenging decision I had ever faced. I had already filed for divorce and was waiting to sign the papers. Now I was walking back into the marriage, but this time, I was clear that fear was not the driving force. I knew family members and friends close to me would not support me. They helped me in leaving. They were not about to support me going back. It did not matter. I had forgiven him, and I had forgiven myself. It was my choice to return and take care of him, not for money or to get what he had. It was my honor to take care of him, to walk out my faith in front of the world. I understood that, but to many, I was the perpetrator—the reason he was sick. If he died, it would be because of me in their eyes. And they told me that to my face.

Some church members told me how much I had hurt them because I did not tell them I was leaving. The Bible says that if your brother has a fault against you, you should go to him and ask for forgiveness. So, I stood before the congregation one Sunday after my husband had passed and made a public apology. It was painful and degrading because I knew they would never understand my pain, and some would never forgive me. I cried all the way home that Sunday.

My attorney informed me that the divorce papers sat in the courthouse for six months, and the clerk could not explain why my case never went to the docket. The answer was God. It was all a part of God's plan. Yes, God told me to leave. Leaving everything familiar behind and stepping into a cloudy future at best was difficult, but it was a part of God's plan for my calling and purpose. My husband left me everything he had, which made many people mad. They did not understand that was his way of asking for forgiveness and trying to make things right.

The doctors told me he had experienced at least three or four mini-strokes. He had stopped taking his medications when they ran out and had not seen his doctors in a year. I did my best to care for him for seven weeks, except for five days in rehab and two days traveling. He needed to be turned every three hours for twenty-four hours a day to avoid more bedsores, and his linen had to be changed three times a day. Family and saints supported me along with the hospice nurses, but at the end of the day and all through the night, it was just me.

Those seven weeks that we were together brought healing to both of our lives. I learned what it means to forgive those who have hurt you the most. I no longer have diabetes, hypertension, or severe sleep apnea. In three years, I had watched my mother, my father, and now my husband die. It hurt. Seeing the humility in his last days, I wished he could live longer, but the crisis was all a part of God's plan for healing in our lives. Do not curse your crisis. God is in it!

My crisis EMPOWERED me to be healed through my pain.

Regan Joseph Llewelyn is a native of Trinidad and Tobago, currently residing in the United Arab Emirates. She has over twenty years of experience working in the medical industry. She holds a Bachelor's degree in Business Management and a Master's degree in Business Administration with an emphasis on Leadership and Innovation. She is the founder and visionary of Philios Women International, birthed out of the need for a safe space and consistent support for women of every nationality and ethnicity to be encouraged and empowered through prayer for their circumstances. She is passionate about evangelism and uses her journey from hurting to healing to helping others. She has served within the church as a leader of the intercessor prayer ministry and is a firm believer in the power of prayer.

Connect with Regan at philioswomeninternational@gmail.com

CRISIS 3

My Path to Restoration

Regan Joseph Llewelyn

I was crashing and burning long before this crisis took place, and my ashes of misery were scattered everywhere, leaving a trail of troubles and tears from all my broken relationships. Sitting in a pool of anxiety, self-criticism, and fear of never finding a suitable partner, I struggled with the constant dread of rejection, which seemed an essential element of my normalcy. I was brokenhearted once again; it was familiar territory. The betrayals, fights, makeups, and breakups were expected, but this time, damn it, it was different!

I lost my part-time hustle. My friends who were always there for me through my relationship dramas were all gone. My family relationships were rocky, and to be honest, I was just a hot mess. At my age, it was not appropriate for life to be so complicated, everything I held on to for comfort was collapsing around me, and I did not know how to fix the wreckage. What I did learn to do was create a façade that everything was okay. Unbeknownst to everyone, I was a lost, hurt, fragile existence in a woman's body.

I got into the car and drove to the airport, about forty-five minutes from where I lived. I had to see him one last time for fear that I would never see him or talk to him again. I kept telling myself I needed closure, but it was more than that. I could not accept that this person had had enough of me and wanted to be done with the relationship. When I arrived at the airport, I was anxious and apprehensive because I could not trust myself. I did not know how I would react if I saw him, but I resolved that I would search until I found him.

I had an idea of his departure time but was still clueless about the flight details. I looked everywhere I could think of and did not see any sign of him. Just when I was about to accept the notion that he had already checked in and gone to his gate, a voice whispered, "Look again." I found new strength to search again; I started back at the place I had previously checked. As I approached the end of the last checkpoint, I spotted Jacob sitting directly in front of me. My heart skipped a million beats of relief and fear. He looked confused and indifferent. "Hi," I said soberly. His face was unmoved. He asked, "What are you doing here?"

I could not verbalize my thoughts and feelings. I had to see him one last time to see if I could salvage what we had. It just felt final, and I could not accept the outcome! To my fortune or misfortune, his flight was delayed. That was the only reason he was sitting there waiting longer than intended to check in and be on his way to his new life in the Middle East, or at least that is how I saw it. I tried to hold back the tears as they welled up inside. My heart was bleeding at the thought of him leaving me behind and ending our romantic relationship, but losing the friendship hurt more. He was so dear to me that I never understood his impact on my life until our friendship was potentially no more. I waited with nothing to say as he sorted out his flight arrangements. He was ready to proceed to the gate. We walked toward the exit as he escorted me outside the building to say our goodbyes.

Feeling that fear of finality bursting from my chest, tears began rolling down my face. I grabbed his coat and cried, making a complete spectacle of myself. Cries of anguish and rejection exploded out of me as I pleaded. "Do not leave me. Please do not go. You promised you would come back for me. You promised!" Passersby looked on as I had an involuntary meltdown. For the first time in my life, I did not care what anyone thought of me. My vulnerabilities were on stage for everyone to see. I loved this man and wanted to fix our relationship. I held onto him for dear life until he also broke down crying. He said repeatedly, "I have to go!" I eventually released his coat with some help from him, and we said our goodbyes.

As I made my way back to the car, dripping wet from walking in the pouring rain and crying my soul out, I could not accept that he was gone; was this the closure I was looking for?

I drove home in the hammering rain and tears that obscured my vision. I was hurting and hopeless. I had another wrecked relationship—another failure to add to my list of failures. No one in my family seemed to have relationship issues of this magnitude. As all the negative thoughts plagued my mind, I was indeed at the end of myself. I could not move past the fact that he had left me, and I was to be blamed; I sank deeper into the abyss of despair. I arrived at the house not knowing that what superseded this event would change my life forever. Weary from all the crying, my eyes swollen and red, I could not think straight. I was so disoriented that I had to call in sick at work. I just kept crying and crying; an indescribable feeling of loss and rejection overshadowed my reasoning. I could not accept that he had left me for his new life and a new adventure!

It was not fair. How could he treat me this way and move on? I felt so used, betrayed, and dejected. The pain intensified as I uttered these words, and so did my wailing. I cried out to God. "Please help me. I do not want to feel this way anymore!" I was emotionally exhausted. I felt so invested and entangled in this relationship. After so many years of making the wrong choices in men and not being able to let go of those toxic relationships, I finally opened myself to someone I thought was good for me. Trying to calm myself proved futile as these indignant thoughts evaded every molecule of my being. My sister gave me a pill to calm my nerves. After the effects kicked in, I had some semblance of composure. I started to pray. I was desperate and frantically in need of help. As I cried out to God, I scrolled through my phone, looking for something relatable on YouTube to distract me from how I felt. I came across a famous preacher sharing the subject "Let It Go!" Those three words lured me in like quicksand, grasping my attention. As I listened intently with tears rolling down my face, I drew strength from what I heard.

I found just enough courage to ask the Lord to help me sincerely. Closely, I heard a soothing voice utter, "Let Jacob go; trust me." I was moved to read 2 Chronicles 20:15-30, the text that embodied the sermon that held my attention. The voice said, "Read this, and hold onto this." It seemed like an assurance for the future, but I could not see past that very moment in time.

Another gentle instruction came as quickly as the one before. "Delete Jacob's number from your phone." Say what now? Was the Lord asking me to do that? Undoubtedly, I was devastated and distressed because this was the only contact information I had for him if I were ever to talk to him again. Indeed, I was not letting go of it! I was still hoping I could salvage our relationship. I heard the command a second time. "Erase Jacob's number from your phone." I was so reluctant and confused. Fear gripped me at the thought of letting him go, but after the third utterance, like a reining ear of a horse, I became attuned to my trainer's voice and painstakingly picked up my phone and deleted his number. I stopped for a minute, contemplating what I had done and the strength and willpower it took to do what I was so exceedingly afraid of—cutting the last connection I had to Jacob.

As I pondered my actions, I did not realize my tears had ceased. Something happened when I submitted to those directives, and my gut-wrenching tears dried up. They were tears from years of hurt, disappointment, rejection, betrayal, shame, and unforgiveness. Every emotion was tucked away in the vault of my heart like precious cargo that slowly devoured my already miserable existence. There was a peace and calmness that easily evaded my thoughts, soul, and spirit like nothing I had ever felt before. Straightaway, I knew God touched me! I had my first night of rest without fear gripping me and triggering anxiety and panic attacks followed by uncontrollable tears. I knew I had to start trusting God and submit to His will if I wanted my life to change for the better. The class was in session!

The voyage of self-discovery was long and painful. It took God almost three years to do a comprehensive transformation in me. Discipline had to become my best friend. I had to embrace what God was doing, but it was not an easy journey; the process confronted and exposed me to the convoluted person I was. It seemed that every time I wanted to press the stop button, God pressed rewind and sent me back to 2 Chronicles 20:15-30 as a reminder of His promise. This passage profoundly impacted my life and made me recognize the magnitude of fear and shame I operated in; it crippled me from letting go of all the people who hurt me and all my mistakes. I did not trust anyone, not even God.

I knew of God and had been in church for most of my young adult life, but this catastrophe with Jacob escorted me right into the open arms of God. God won my attention. In my quest to understand myself, God had to disclose countless things: my insecurities, pride, anger, shame, and bitterness. He even uncovered my unforgiveness toward so many folks, including my father. He abandoned me when I was nine years old, which may have been one of the major precursors for my desperately wrong choices in men and the need for their love and attention. As I quickly gravitated to the word of God for help, I was challenged to introspect, be obedient, and accept corrections. The modifications were gradual but unquestionably necessary. A time of healing began. A time of pruning and loneliness began. Let us talk about that loneliness for a minute. That emotion flooded my soul fast and furiously. I was still so afraid I would end up alone—without a man and a husband. Frequently, loneliness would raise its dreadful head, which triggered thoughts of rejection.

I became so broken and discouraged. "But God," I exclaimed! "You told me You would do it for me." What was this "it" God was going to do? As I crumbled before God, He was so gracious to converse with me, comfort me, and encourage me. In one instance, I went to Him in tears. Remember, this journey was almost three years, so naturally, like anyone, I questioned if God had forgotten me. He and I would have this conversation again. I was back asking God when it would all end. When would I get married and have all the beautiful things, He promised me? I needed radical faith, so God led me to read all the promises. He guided me to journal during our dialogues for times when I felt so unstable.

As I read my journal, He guided me back to what I had written some months prior. "Jacob will return home in December this year and ask you to get married." God knew the desire of my heart. He knew I still hoped for that relationship to be restored, but He also knew I had to surrender my heart to Him. Even if it were not going to be Jacob, I had to believe and accept it would be whom God found fit and deserving for me. I said, "Okay, God," leaning on every ounce of faith I could muster at this point. Now in retrospect, God allowed this situation to draw me closer to Him, helping me see myself in the light of His love. God knew how to fix my longing for love!

I took a deep breath, accepted the path I was on, and started to channel my energy and focus on self-improvement. I learned to love and accept myself. I learned to embrace and enjoy my singleness. I learned to value relationships, and most of all, I had encounters with God that changed my life forever. I was joyful and pleasant to be around, sentiments uttered by my mother, who knew the miserable person she lived with. I learned to enjoy the presence of God and the sweet fellowship we developed as I pursued His love and not the love of a man. I welcomed the new and improved version of myself. Physical, emotional, mental, and spiritual rebuilding took place inside out. The façade was replaced by a deep conviction and resolve that no man or thing could refute.

Life felt good, and I had let go of all my inhibitions and started to live a life of purpose and expectancy. On my way home one afternoon, I received an unexpected but welcome phone call. It was Jacob. At first, I did not realize it, but as we spoke, I felt comfortable. We spoke briefly; from then on, the conversations were more frequent, and it felt new like we were getting to know each other all over again. God did a new thing! When God does a thing, He does it with excellence and purpose. What He said unfolded. Jacob returned from abroad in December of that year, planned our wedding date without my knowledge, and asked me to get married, which we did six months before I relocated to the Middle East.

When I recall the events that led me to this place in my life, I am in awe of how quickly everything unfolded as God reminded me that my latter days would be greater than my former days. I am ever so grateful for what I endured to become a woman of faith and conviction, a good wife, a better daughter, sister, friend, and a vessel for God's use. My crisis led me to one act of obedience brought restoration that changed my life forever. There is a purpose in everything we experience. Even our marriage has been stamped to be an example to other unions, which we live out daily.

My crisis EMPOWERED me to overcome broken relationships.

Zandra Sims is a native of Chesapeake, Virginia; she and her husband, Dennis, have been married for over thirty years. They are proud parents of three adult sons, Leon, Dondrae, and Russell, and thirteen grandchildren. She received her undergraduate degree from Old Dominion University, Master of Arts in Rehabilitation Counseling from Norfolk State University, and Certificate of Advanced Studies in Educational Leadership from The George Washington University. She is currently working on a Doctor of Ministry degree at Virginia Union University. Zandra is a licensed minister, Adjunct Professor and has been an educator for over twenty-five years within mental health facilities, public school systems, and the collegiate level. Her licensed teaching area focuses on students with disabilities as well as college students who desire basic skills in the counseling profession. Zandra believes her faith and family are most important in her life.

Connect with Zandra at zandrasims@yahoo.com

CRISIS 4

Thirteen and Counting

Zandra Sims

-✠-✠-✠-✠-✠-✠-✠-

Alone, unsure, and in an ambulance with two strangers, "What in the world are they going to do to me?" I thought. The tears had already started to build up in the corners of my eyes. I knew they would be released soon as my eyes began to burn. It was April 23, 1984—Easter Monday. I remember it like it was yesterday. It was a muggy, sweltering misty day, and rain splashed on my face. The people positioned me in the ambulance.

There I was—a scrawny little Black girl in a predicament that most adult women are prepared, excited, and eager to experience. I was petrified and did not understand what was getting ready to transpire. I did not even comprehend the magnitude of emotional and physical pain I was about to endure. Apprehension, fear, abandonment, rejection, loneliness, and the desire to be a people-pleaser took root and grew at an accelerated rate in my heart. The emotions roamed in my mind at a level that most 13-year-olds would never experience or imagine.

Each feeling had its own identity and compartment within me, but shame was the one I picked up and carried with me. I slept with it, ate, talked, and even went to school with it. I carried it as if it were part of me. The shame was attached to my skin, and I owned it. The trauma of this experience would be devastating to me.

Nurses and doctors I had never met were running in and out of the hospital room caring for me, but some wanted to see—put their eyes on—the 13-year-old clueless little girl who was about to deliver a baby. They were working frantically to position my fragile, thin body to prepare me for an unimaginable procedure that would forever alter my life—the life of a child already living in poverty. The tears streaming down my face were mute to those in the room but sounded like drums from a marching band in my ear. The shame gripped me so that my eyes were bonded together. I thought that would force the doctors and nurses to enter the room as if I were transparent.

Click, clack, bang, bang—the birthing equipment terrorized me even more, causing my fear and anxiety to leap. But the sounds that disturbed me the most were the voices of the nurses and doctors. The comments that many made ripped my weak heart into a thousand more little pieces.

I could not believe I was hearing statements such as, "Where is her mother?" No one knows. She should be ashamed of herself. These fast girls nowadays! Do not make any sense! They said her mother was in a hotel room. Has anyone tried to contact the parent? There are more and more young girls who end up in this situation. They are project girls. This is so sad. I do not know why she is over there, sad and crying. She laid down to make it like a grown woman. Let her deal with the pain. This makes no sense. "Where is her mother? No one can contact her, sir. Well, we will have to take the baby. We can no longer wait for the mother to arrive." I could not believe I was hearing all this from those assigned to care for me at such a critical time in my adolescent life.

In my mind, I replied, "Take the baby." I yelled out from deep within, "NO, DON'T TAKE MY BABY!" I cried profusely until my body shook like a leaf on a tree during a winter storm. Suddenly, a nurse came over, patting my arm and speaking quietly, asking, "What's wrong, baby?" I explained, taking a deep breath between every spoken word. "Please do not do it. I do not want anyone to take my baby away." I promised the nurse that if they let me keep my baby, I would not do it again. I begged them not to take my baby away and apologized for having sex. As I think about it now, I smile with disbelief and shake my head at how oblivious I was to the entire labor and delivery procedure. But then again, I should have been. After all, I was a 13-year-old child.

The nurse clarified what the doctors were preparing to do. They were going to perform a medical procedure called a cesarean section, a c-section for short. She explained that doctors opt for this procedure when a woman cannot have a baby by natural birth through the vagina. Instead, the woman births the baby through the stomach area. I took a deep breath of relief. As I exhaled, I looked at the nurse, smiled, and thanked her. Although I was still a little confused, I was pleased they would not take my baby away from me.

I heard heart-wrenching comments that no child should ever hear. I was still alone, and the tears flowed for hours. I had to listen to the demeaning, condescending, harsh, loud whispers about my mom and me. In the back of my mind, I wondered if my boyfriend and baby's father, Leon, would ever arrive to be with us. "Where is he?" I thought. "Is anyone coming to help me?" The longer I was there with no one, the more the shame grew and took over all of me.

We were two young, naïve kids who made pitiful choices and poor decisions, trying to follow the crowd. We were still together and vowed never to break up. Little did we know that was a fictitious dream. We did not understand that life as we knew it was no more. It vanished, disappeared, and washed away forever. Now, what would we do?

Eventually, the same thing happened to our relationship. We grew apart daily, and the relationship had run its course. It was over, and we would never be reunited again. The most significant treasure of our relationship was my strong little football player, Leon. He has always displayed a nonchalant attitude, as nothing bothers him.

While in the hospital room, I longed to see a familiar face. Finally, Ms. Joyce, Leon's mother, arrived. In addition to being the grandmother of my unborn child, she became my teacher, my caregiver, and the mother that was not my biological mother. She had always treated me as one of her children, allowing me to be at their house on many occasions. When Ms. Joyce found out I was pregnant, she was one of the few who did not reject me or make me feel like an outsider. I loved Ms. Joyce. So, when she walked into the cold hospital room, my face lit up like fireworks on a 4th of July night. Our eyes connected and spoke volumes in silence. I was so relieved that her presence, which demands respect and attention, allowed me to attach sounds to my tears, and I cried out like a trumpet. Finally, I thought to myself, "Someone I know and loves me is here."

Ms. Joyce's presence always controlled the atmosphere without any spoken words. Long after my relationship with her son ended, she loved all my children and me. I thank her for always loving us unconditionally. As soon as she walked into the hospital room that day, the doctors and nurses discontinued their undesirable and cruel comments. Although Ms. Joyce had arrived, deep down inside, I longed for my mother to shelter me from words, cutting my self-esteem and heart down to nothing.

I could not see my baby immediately after delivery. The doctors decided I needed to sleep during the c-section, so I was sent to recovery right after he was born. I developed excessive swelling and an abnormal blood pressure rate, so I was only allowed to see my son for a few moments when I woke up. They laid him on my chest for three short minutes. I could barely lift my arms to hold him or hand him to the nurse. I did not expect the nurse to come and whisk him off so abruptly. I felt like a woman in bondage during slavery who got her child snatched away without permission. Then the crying started all over again.

Later that night, I was finally fully awake and able to hold my son. Leon was 7 pounds, 5 ounces and 23 1/2 inches long. He was so cute, and his eyes opened when I looked at him. I was so excited to see him. This beautiful little boy came from me. Wow, I could not believe it. I was overwhelmed with joy yet frightened, thinking about what would happen next. Not knowing what was next was very unsettling and troubling.

A day later, loud sounds interrupted my sleep. It was my mother's raging voice. "Where is my daughter?" she asked as she wandered the hospital's halls. I was distressed and in a delicate state that I could not explain then but can put into words now. I was overcome with discomfort and trauma. My time as a child would vanish forever, and I had no choice but to quickly, and I mean quickly, grow up.

A year and a half later, I asked myself how I got into a new situation. There I was again, understanding and knowing the consequences of my behaviors. Why was I so stupid not to use protection? I did not know what to do. There were no excuses for me. I did not want to go through the whispers, name-calling, abandonment, rejection, separation, and shame. The shame grew, causing me to think less of whom God had called me to become. "What can I do? What can I do? How can I get an abortion? Maybe I will get rid of this baby." Then I will not have to deal with any of the backlashes.

But I could not do it, so I released that thought to the wind. His father and I met while I was visiting my aunt. Again, trouble was on the horizon, and the relationship ended as soon as it started. The greatest thing from that relationship was my little busy baseball slugger, Dondrae. He is the sensitive and hardworking one.

On December 3, 1985, I went into labor. Because of the tightness inside my body, I did not dilate much. I experienced less pain and was ridiculed by hospital staff as my doctor decided that another cesarean section would be the wisest choice for my body. Dondrae was born weighing 6 ½ pounds and 8 ounces. He was one of the smallest babies in the nursery but had the biggest smile. As a baby, he smiled all the time.

At the time, my self-perception was so damaging. I filled my mind with derogatory statements about what I thought others felt about me. I realized that self-perception could become the encourager or the murderer. I thought about committing suicide on multiple occasions. School saved my life because it was my refuge and haven. It was the fertile place where I needed to cultivate my life. There, I received affirmation and approval from my teachers. They always told me there was greatness in me. I could be a child for a few hours out of the day. It was the safest place for me. I excelled and pushed myself beyond my expectations. Understanding that being in school was only going to last for a few hours per day, I soaked in every moment and acquired everything I could get while I was there.

As the end of the school day approached, my mind and body started transitioning back to motherhood. My attitude would change from being an excited and enthusiastic student to becoming a young mother with two small children, constantly looking for my way in life and wondering if I was making the right decisions.

Quite often, when I arrived home, I started thinking about my potential based on my academic performance. I realized it was time to start applying what I knew was on the inside of me. Although we were not the average church family, I understood God must have been with me to get me that far. So, I developed the resilience needed to promote a more positive mindset and attitude. I reminded myself and replayed the video of the encouraging words from my teachers and cousins, who were more like brothers and sisters. They supported me in being the best I could be.

Through all the trauma in my life, I understood that shame held me back the most. It crippled my thoughts and held me captive in a cage of anger and resentment toward anyone I felt mistreated me. Once I let go and scraped the cords of shame off my mind, I began to flourish and believe in myself. I wanted more and to do better regardless of what it took. I realized I had a support system that fueled my fire to start a movement. My crisis empowered me to realize that God was with me even though I made some negative choices and did not have a supportive family at home. Even if nobody else loved me, God did. The shape of my identity changed, and I know that having a positive mindset can help your identity blow away the lies you have believed about yourself. I learned to love myself the way God loves me, and from that, I can love my husband, Dennis, and my children, Leon, Dondrae, and Russell.

**My crisis EMPOWERED me to
eradicate the shame of negative
choices and thoughts.**

Ricardo and Kimberly Frost are multiple award winners, business owners, and Founders of RFK Solutionz Corporation, a Cyber Security Services and Training company. RFK was named Small Business of the Year for Chesapeake, Virginia, in 2019. It provides cutting-edge Cyber Security Training to the federal government and corporations globally. RFK Solutionz is most proud of its yearly Cyber Security Academy for local kids ages 11 – 17, and in 2021 hosted a multi-state cyber academy held in Brevard County, Florida. Ricardo and Kimberly both retired from the U.S. Navy as Chief Petty Officers after twenty years of Honorable service in Information Technology (Surface Warfare/Air Warfare). Ricardo received his Bachelor's degree in Technical Management with a concentration in Security from DeVry University. Kimberly received her Bachelor's degree in Workforce Education and Development from Southern Illinois University and a double Master's degree, with Distinction, from Keller Graduate School of Management. The "With Distinction" was awarded to Kimberly for persevering and continuing her Master's degree while recovering from ovarian cancer. Ricardo and Kimberly are passionate about serving the community through outreach initiatives. They believe that to be successful, you must first be a servant (Matthew 23:11). Their commitment to giving people a hand up, not out, shows through their efforts in educating through marriage conferences, veteran and homeless outreach events, and local community activities. They serve through their registered 501 (c)(3) nonprofit ministry, Redemption. They are licensed Ministers at The Mount Global Fellowship of Churches in VA. Ricardo and Kimberly have been married for over twenty years; they have two adult children, Raymond and Rayven, one son-in-love, Jose Jackson, and three grandchildren, Jett, Jade, and Jayden.

Connect with Ricardo and Kimberly at www.RFKOutreach.com

CRISIS 5

It Was Hidden

Ricardo and Kimberly Frost

"I'm the top cancer doctor in this hospital, but you don't have cancer!" This was the statement made by the lead oncologist surgeon to Kimberly and me in the surgical operating room. This statement changed the trajectory of our lives from what we wanted to what was intended. It came after the rollercoaster ride of emotions and uncertainties that my wife had experienced throughout this medical crisis. Prior to this surgery date, we had spoken with several medical professionals, including her primary care doctor. The primary care doctor informed my wife that she was suffering from what she believed to be fibroid tumors in her uterus. Kimberly's doctor was not a specialist, so she sent a referral to a so-called expert in the field of gynecological studies. The more familiar term is GYN. My wife was desperately seeking assistance from these doctors to help her identify and remove the pain and discomfort she had been experiencing for over twelve months! Seeking help from doctor after doctor to no avail brought me to the remembrance of a famous no-name Bible character, "the woman with the issue of blood." I could see the hope of relief slowly eroding like beach sand from the high and low tide in my wife's heart, and there was nothing I could do physically to remove the pain. As a husband, there is nothing worse than not being able to be the "Superman" that you think your wife expects you to be. I had to learn to pray and trust God during a time when my hands were useless, but my faith was necessary!

Retiring from the United States Navy was an achievement that I will never forget. Twenty years of service to my country was a goal I had planned from age nineteen. I knew from the day I enlisted that I would remain on active duty until I was eligible for retirement. A few years before my naval retirement, I felt a powerful desire to start a business and become an entrepreneur. The nerve of me to have that type of vision when no one in my family had ever started a business before, so I had no one to call nor lean on when it came to developing the plan for the company. That did not stop me from pressing forward with the vision. I was all alone in this process because Ricardo was still on active duty for another four years and would not be able to offer much support with the development of this business. The vision that had been given was to develop a Cyber Security business that would be aligned with teaching teenagers and young adults how to certify and obtain employment in the field of Cyber Security. It was an exciting plan, but I learned early that it was not an easy one. Starting a business, as I had planned, did not work out at that time. I desired to connect with the Economic Development Director for the city where I resided, find a building space to purchase or rent, and jump feet-first into training individuals in Cyber Security. That plan did not work at all. In my mind, I had failed not only myself and my family but also God's vision and purpose for my life. I had not done enough research, nor did I know enough about starting a business to get it off the ground successfully. I reluctantly gave up and secured a job working for the federal government. God indeed set up the position I secured, but at the time of hire, I was unaware He was orchestrating my footsteps.

Five years have passed since I started my federal position. Ricardo had retired and was home enjoying his break after retirement. We had a decent income between the two of us, and we were in no hurry to change our cost or comfort of living. "We were living our life like it was golden, living our life like it was golden," just like the words in Jill Scott's song. We enjoyed traveling, serving in our local church, and waiting for our last child to graduate. You could not tell us that we were not living a good life. Our marriage was on autopilot, and we were in love. As I started to round out year five of retirement, working my comfortable job in Cyber, one morning, I was lying in bed next to Ricardo having pillow talk after a time of intimacy. I shared with him that morning, "Baby, I am having so much pain in my body, and I have no idea what could be causing this pain that I am experiencing day in and day out. My menstrual cycle was out of control, and the cramps became unbearable." I shared with him that I was using the bathroom more than usual, and based on the lab test results, there was no infection. I was dying slowly on the inside. I scheduled appointment after appointment at the Veteran's hospital (VA) with my primary care doctor and several specialists. Still, my doctor at the VA continuously shared with me that I just needed to lose weight, and I would feel better. At that time, I had gained a tremendous amount of weight. I was tipping the scales of three hundred pounds, but I knew it was more than that. The VA doctor's words would cause me to leave his office upset and in tears because I did not believe he was taking my concerns seriously. I knew my weight was not the problem as he had stated. I was sure that it was much more than that. Ricardo was so supportive and caring. He prayed with me, and together we began to get more aggressive with finding answers for my medical issue with the hopes of receiving an accurate diagnosis. Instead of seeking medical doctors for a diagnosis, we began to seek God in prayer. "Kimberly, you have cancer" were the words I heard in prayer one morning. I said, "CANCER." While I continued to pray, I could feel despair trying to get into my mind. I could feel life leaving me as I believed God had just shared with me that I had cancer. I figured He was telling me this so that I could stop worrying and start planning for my new future. A future that included an early death sentence. By the time I got off my knees, I had planned out my entire funeral: the colors I would wear were all white. I selected which of my sisters would help care for my young adult children after I had gone to glory. Would Ricardo be able to move on without me? Would he remarry? The thought of him remarrying shifted my thinking to how I would be able to haunt him and his new wife so that they would have absolutely no peace as husband and wife, jokingly.

I continued to think, would he have children with her? Would she be younger, prettier, fine as wine? All these thoughts raced through my mind in all of thirty seconds but seemed more like hours. Then I remembered snapping out of the moment and started to rebuke everything about hearing those words. I told myself I would be darned if another huzzy would take my place with my husband, live in my house, and raise my kids. I shifted my thinking and began to refuse to believe it, but I was sure God was sharing my diagnosis with me.

I started to believe He was sharing those words with me so that I could stop seeking a diagnosis and begin seeking a solution for my issue and not plan for my demise. I shifted gears in my faith. From that day forward, I began to grab ahold of every time I heard someone praying for healing. I am healed is what I would repeat. I would cry to God, "I am healed by your stripes Lord." That is what your word says, and I will hold you to your promises." I refused to give up on myself. I had too much to live for. My daughter still had to graduate high school; she needed me to be there after she finished college. Who was going to help her with her wedding dress and her children? Who would be there to help my son choose the right wife and teach him how to lead his family? I needed to live, and you can best believe that my faith and belief system went into overdrive! I was going to live! I claimed my healing before receiving a confirmed diagnosis from a certified doctor. During this part of the journey, I was alone in my faith because I had not shared with Ricardo or my family the dream that revealed my diagnosis. I knew that Ricardo would have thoroughly rebuked the dream in its entirety, so it was best for me to keep the dream to myself.

As the months went by and Kimberly did not seem to be getting any better, I began to worry, but the strange thing was I never feared her dying or living without her. I always believed that she would be fine. I knew she was in constant pain and was depressed, but I felt that losing weight and our faith in God's promises would be all she would need to overcome this crisis. In my mind, I thought that it would be just that simple. During that time in our lives, we were serving a great deal in our church, and we had true ride-or-die prayer partners that God used to help us when we got weak in our faith. There was no way that God would take Kimberly away from me and the kids! We had much that still needed to be done! I was retiring from the military and could finally realize a life with her and my children that did not include moving every three to four years. I dreamt of a life where I no longer had to leave them to go on deployment for six-plus months at a time. I envisioned a world where I no longer had to worry about duty days, leaving them alone in the house and not being there to protect them if there were break-ins or any other catastrophe that could happen to them and leave me devastated for the rest of my life! I thought this was a test we had the answers to in our lives. I thought we were diligent students in ministry, family, and faith, but God gave us a pop quiz in the school of life for which we were unprepared.

In the summer of 2011, Tricare benefit representative stated, "The military medical system recognized that you are being bounced around from doctor to doctor." The representative asked, "Would you be willing to visit the Naval hospital for treatment?" After seeing many different doctors and specialists, I reluctantly accepted the appointment at the Naval hospital. My reluctance was due to the reputation that the local Naval hospital. The word was that you would check in with a jammed toe and never check out. That is a genuine belief that service members carried at that time. After a great deal of thought, I called the representative back, and she made me an appointment with the oncology doctor who was a resident in the gynecology department.

Tests were run, and the results were that I had a fibroid tumor in my uterus that was the size of an eight-pound baby. The specialist believed that the fibroid tumor was causing me the discomfort I had been experiencing over the past twelve months. The specialist suggested to Ricardo and me that we consider having a partial hysterectomy to remove the massive tumor and restore my health. Ricardo, without hesitation, stated, "Let's do it if this will give Kimberly relief." I was not as quick to respond because I knew this would end any opportunity for Ricardo and me to conceive a baby together. We asked the doctor to give us time to talk about it and pray. We came to the best decision for my well-being, remove the uterus. Ricardo sacrificed the gift of a biological child for the gift of restoring my health.

Once we connected with the GYN specialist at the Naval hospital, and he explained what he believed was happening with Kimberly, I was relieved because he seemed confident in his diagnosis. I was thrilled that we had finally gotten someone who knew what he was diagnosing and had tangible proof to show us what was happening with Kimberly's body. He never made snap judgments based on Kimberly's physical appearance; he did the work and the research! This gave me a whole new perspective on the less-than-stellar reputation that this hospital was known for. After the detailed research of the GYN specialist, he informed us that my wife had a fibroid tumor in her uterus that was the size of an eight-pound baby! He also informed us that her body was responding to the tumor as if it were a baby adjusting to give birth. This explained the lack of a consistent menstrual cycle and the continued weight gain. What a difference someone who cares makes! He informed us that he would have to perform surgery as soon as possible and that it would be a good possibility that he may have to perform a partial hysterectomy on Kimberly to ensure that he was able to remove the entire tumor and get Kimberly on the road to recovery. After hearing this news, I was ready for him to proceed without any reservations. Kimberly was not as quick to approve of the surgery. You see, it was not that she did not want the surgery; the problem was that as great as our family was with our amazing children, Kimberly knew that I did not have any biological children of my own. She wanted to bless me with a biological child. I had problems producing children due to my medical issues with infertility. I had tried fertility treatments in the past with no success, but we never gave up hope of the possibility that God would bless us with a child created by the two of us. This procedure would truly end our hopes of having a baby. Kimberly had second thoughts about having surgery that would help bring her out of her twelve months of misery and uncertainty to have the opportunity to have a child for me. Wow! Even as I write about this years later, the emotion that I feel for her willingness to sacrifice her health for the sake of having a baby for me still impacts me like being punched in the stomach; it takes my breath away! Knowing how she thought about this moment played a huge mind trick in how I would respond when I had to make a life-or-death decision for her.

It was surgery day, and Kimberly and me were in the prep room praying and sharing words of encouragement when a doctor walked in with those life-altering words: "I'm the top cancer doctor in this hospital, but you don't have cancer!" He informed us that he was fascinated by the abnormal size of Kimberly's tumor and that he just had to be part of the surgery. At this very moment, God showed Kimberly and me that He truly knows our end from our beginning! I never knew that Kimberly had cancer, but God did, and He placed the best doctor in the hospital in her operating room! He would take over the surgery because of his experience and expertise. While Kimberly was still open on the operating table, he left the surgery to inform me that Kimberly would have to have a total hysterectomy resulting in the removal of both ovaries! He stated that he could leave the one tumor-free ovary but believed that in a few years cancer would appear in the remaining ovary and take Kimberly's life. This is the moment I was referring to when talking about the life-or-death decision I had to make for Kimberly. Usually, I would have made this decision without hesitation; the problem was the very last words that Kimberly spoke to me before they rolled her into the operating room were," Please do not let them take my ovaries."

My eyes opened after surgery and standing around my bed was my family. Instead of having excitement on their faces, they had looks of despair. I know my family, and it is not much that they can hide from me. I asked them if everything was ok, and they smiled and said everything was fine. My analytical mind started racing back to the fact that I woke up in the recovery room eight hours after my surgery start time vice the two-and-a-half hours we were told the surgery would take. At that moment, I realized something did not go according to plan. Ricardo saw that I was starting to get suspicious of their responses and for my surgeon to visit me. The surgeon that appeared was not the surgeon I was assigned to when I went for the procedure. Instead, it was that doctor who walked in right before they rolled me back for the procedure, announcing that he was the top cancer doctor in the hospital. Remember, he said, "You do not have cancer, but your tumor is so large I want to be a part of this procedure to witness and assist your surgeon if needed." Well, guess what? When they opened me up, they removed the uterus with success. As they did a once-over inside my pelvic area, they noticed that I had a lot of scar tissue inside of me from a prior surgery that was blocking them from seeing my ovaries and tubes. The assigned surgeon began to remove the scar tissue so that he could see my ovaries; And low and behold, when he viewed my ovary, it was huge. The oncologist knew immediately that it had a tumor growing inside of it and that it was probably cancerous and at any moment would rupture. He shared with us that the cosmetic surgery I had years earlier had caused a massive amount of internal scar tissue; the scar tissue from that surgery had encapsulated the ovary. God encapsulated the ovary with the scar tissue to prevent it from bursting and killing me. "Ok, can we take a praise break?" Listen, he said my life had been spared because of cosmetic surgery I had had ten years earlier. Talk about God turning your bad decisions around for your good. The surgeon shared that the ovary would have ruptured within six months, and I would have succumbed to ovarian cancer. But God! Not only did he find cancer in stage 1A, but I also did not have to endure radiation or chemotherapy! Statistically, during that time, two in ten women survived ovarian cancer. One of those two ladies will live an additional five years. It has been eleven years, and I am a miracle. God saw fit for me to be the one in ten to survive the silent killer called ovarian cancer. God is so amazing! Remember, He informed me almost six months earlier that I had cancer during prayer time with Him. He had already arranged my healing long before my cancer was confirmed. He diverted me from the civilian medical providers to the local Naval hospital. He then sent in the top oncologist at the Naval hospital just moments before I was to go back for surgery. At that time, no one knew I had cancer except God himself. The doctor informed my family that if he had not been in the operating room during that surgery, the doctor would have closed me back up and missed that tumor. I cry with deep emotion every time I share this testimony. Ricardo and I were radical for Christ before my healing, but this special touch by God took our walk to an entirely new level. Our FAITH level in God is unmeasurable!

Three months passed, and my doctor released me to return to work for the federal government. I realized after my return that my life was not the same. I realized that God had orchestrated our crisis to get us back on track for what He had called us to accomplish and to be a testimony for His Glory. God reminded me that He had given me a vision and a purpose before I retired from the navy, and that was to start our business which would open the door to marketplace ministry for the two of us. Soon after that reminder, I submitted my resignation and walked away from my job in faith to make a second attempt at starting our Cyber Security business. This time, God instilled wisdom and knowledge in me over the five years I worked. Now, I could start the business successfully with the additional skills I had earned. The first time I launched out was too soon. It was not time. God had given me the vision, but it was for Ricardo and me to manage together.

Today we celebrate ten years in business and have earned awards along the way, including Small Business of the Year for our city, and I received an award as a Women of Honor and Entrepreneur of the Year. We were also licensed as ministers of the gospel. Ricardo and I learned that God's timing is not our timing; His plans are not our plans, and His ways are not ours. God orchestrated His plan for us in Cyber Security and positioned us as marketplace ministers for the Kingdom. This feat may have never happened if we had cursed our crisis.

**Our crisis EMPOWERED us to
become global business owners.**

Kecia Lawrence is an anointed author, teacher, speaker, consultant, and minister. She was born and raised in Baltimore, Maryland, the youngest of three, and is the mother of three. Kecia is a retired 20-year Army veteran. She believes education is essential. She attended parochial school from pre-kindergarten to eighth grade and completed her primary education at the prestigious all-girls school, Western High. She is an alum of Bluefield College, Virginia, with a Bachelor of Science in Organizational Management and Leadership, and Regent University with an MBA with a concentration in Entrepreneurship. Kecia is the founder and CEO of Empowered to Live by Design, LLC (ELD) birthed through her desire to be a champion for other women. Kecia endeavors to bring understanding to unhealthy behaviors in relationships that too often devastate lives. She is passionate about providing positive insight and reinforcement to women so that they may obtain success spiritually, personally, professionally, and financially.

Connect with Kecia at Empoweredtolivebydesign@gmail.com

CRISIS 6

Depression Was Not My Friend

Kecia L. Lawrence

A series of traumatic events spiraled me downward into a hole of depression so deep and dark that I did not know if I would ever be able to climb out. An abusive alcoholic father, two abortions, two miscarriages, molestation by two uncles, and two divorces left me on the Emotional Wellness floor of a psychiatric ward.

The departure of my second husband was the proverbial straw that broke the camel's back. I finally cracked under the weight of a lifetime of shame, rejection, and abandonment. It was six months from when he said he was divorcing me until he actually left. It hit me so hard because after he told me the first time he wanted to leave, there was calm in the house. No more arguing. No more tension. Just a lot of niceties. I prayed. I fasted. I read marriage enrichment books. I thought it was getting better, but that day still came.

It was Valentine's Day! He prepaid for a romantic couple's package with dinner, roses, and a hotel on the beach. I was so excited. I thought he had changed his mind. The day he told me he was still leaving was a punch in my gut. Temporary insanity came over me. Questions and thoughts of disbelief plagued me. This could not be. Things had gotten better. We were getting along. How can he leave? He said he loved me. We agreed to take divorce off the table when we got married. I do not understand. What is happening?

That morning, it took all I had to get my younger children off to school and my oldest child to work. I then mindlessly drove to my therapist's office. After a mere few minutes in a session, she called to secure a place for me in the Emotional Wellness Center. This was the beginning of the end of a lifetime of misery. I felt as if I had an out-of-body experience. It was as if I was looking down at myself, hearing and seeing what was happening but somehow disconnected. A joint counseling session was scheduled during my first days of admission. I remember telling him that he had broken me. He told me that I was broken when we met. The truth of his words rocked me to my core. The depression, pain, and insecurity were there long before we met.

The last question I remember the therapist asking is, "Are you willing to work on the marriage?" He said, "No." My entire body became flushed. It felt as if I had been dropped into an inferno. I stood up. My head was swirling. I felt nauseous. I stumbled out of that office as all my strength left my body. I clung to the hallway wall until I could no longer stand. I slid down the wall onto the hard marble floor. Like the sound of a wounded animal, a high-pitched howl came out of me as I slumped over. The sound was shocking, unearthing, and a sweet release, all at the same time. All the pain and abuse I stuffed down for years in order to survive refused to stay suppressed. I had to start unpacking, which is now called "doing the work."

My old friend, depression, showed up in full force. He was never far away. From an early age, he was always there; lulling me to sleep; keeping me away from others; forbidding connection to others; a low-lying pain ready to hit ten at any moment. I had never questioned him before. I never asked why he was there. He was just a part of me that became my norm. The psychiatrist diagnosed me with Dissociative Disorder. As defined by Mayo Clinic, Dissociative Disorder states that people with this mental disorder experience disconnection and lack of continuity between thoughts, memories, surroundings, actions, and identity. This disorder enables one to escape reality by disassociating with emotions or painful stimuli. The disconnection is involuntary and unhealthy, which causes problems functioning in everyday life.

I coined a term to describe how I lived; "functional depressant." I unknowingly mastered the art of emotionally disconnecting from anyone or anything that could hurt me. I was the "never let them see you sweat girl," and the "get it done by any means necessary." Old reliable! This competent, well-educated, jack-of-all-trades persona became my mask and coping mechanism. People began to equate who I was with what I could accomplish. I excelled at whatever I put my hands on but was broken and bruised inside. Work became my language of love; however, I recognized this was just a different form of abuse. I felt used but not loved. Accomplished but not accepted.

Not only was I a functional depressant, but I also mastered "emotional cutting." After years of disappointment, I learned not to rely on others. I refused to let anyone get close enough to my heart to hurt me. I cut people off physically and emotionally. I lived by the rule that if I did not expect anything from anyone, no one would have the power to hurt or disappoint me. I became the master of my own emotions. I willed it. Whether it was laughter or tears, I decided if I would or would not experience it.

Depression is painful and robs us of the relationships we crave and the life we deserve. Many days I laid on the floor crying out for help. The only words I could utter were "oh God" over and over and over. I knew He was the only one that could help me.

Sleep became my drug of choice. When I felt I could not cope, I slept; but sleep could never remove the images of my mother curled up in a ball on the floor near the basement door as my father kicked and stomped her. Sleep could not make me forget the lecherous look of my uncles nor their weight on my tiny body as they held me to the ground. Sleep turned into nightmares when I thought of the cruelty and inhumane acts of the two abortions I underwent. Sleep did help me to momentarily forget the two miscarriages I had. It helped me stop thinking I did not deserve them or anything else good to happen to me anyway. When the waters of life overwhelmed me, my old friend depression would say, "Sleep." It took a long time to realize that depression did not want me to go to sleep. It wanted me to stay asleep.

The birth of my oldest son was a gift, a lifeboat from God. I needed a reason to live, something greater than myself to care for, but even the gift of my son came with a price. My first marriage was at the age of twenty-two. It was doomed before it started. We met in Europe, a place where realities are set aside. When we returned to the states, it was like, what did we do? It was not long before some young girl down the street caught his eye. We became less and less intimate until we never touched each other. One day he decided he wanted to sleep with me just one more time. I am sure this test was the determining factor. If the sex were good, he would stay. If not, then it was time to move on. I had been off my contraceptive. I asked him to wait, but he was on a mission. We were lying on that floor with him on top of me. I lay there lifeless, thinking how familiar this felt. I remember thinking I want this to be over. I felt the conception happen. I knew I was pregnant before I got up. He never touched me again after that night. Nine months later, my son was born. One day depression said, "I wish I could lay on this couch and never wake up," but another voice said, "Get up. Your son needs you."

I honestly cannot ever remember being happy. The traumas started at such an early age. I grew up in the inner city of East Baltimore. My father was my hero before the monster took his place. My fondest memory of him is walking me to Pre-K. He sat in his easy chair with his white starched Coca-Cola shirt and green uniform pants while I sat on the plastic-covered couch. When *Bewitch* went off, he stood up, took me by my hand, and walked me the mile to school. We did this like clockwork. I never remember exchanging words, just a goodbye wave as he watched me walk up the marble steps of the school.

The loving father I once adored became consumed with alcohol and rage. There was no rhyme or reason for his abusive tirade, just that they became increasingly frequent. He was particularly abusive and offensive to my brother because he was brave enough to try to help my mom. Unlike me, who cowered in fear, I could only stand and watch in silence and horror as he threatened to kill her with guns, punches, and stomp on her. My inability to help or even call out has tortured me my entire life. It produced feelings in me that I could not understand. I hated myself and my mom but never "the monster." I hated myself for being the coward and her for being the victim.

Things got so dangerous that my mom, siblings, and I went to live with my grandmom in another state. It was jumping out of the frying pan into the fire. My parents sent us off to stay with our grandparents over the summer to "keep us safe." I suffered many years of inappropriate touching, groping, and being pinned down. My grandmom had one bathroom down a long hallway that lasted forever. I always seem to get trapped in the backroom. I tried to time myself to ensure I did not go back there when others were not around, but sometimes, I would forget. My uncle, fifteen years older, would throw me on the floor. He grabbed me by my wrist and pinned them beside my head on either side. The memory of his weight on my body and the look in his eyes made me sick to my stomach. I wanted to scream, but my brain would not allow me. After what seemed like an eternity, he would let me go. I hated myself for letting myself get caught up time after time. I would ask, "What's wrong with you?" A question I had asked myself my entire life was, "What is wrong with you?" I never told anyone. I reasoned that if I told anyone, my father would kill both of my uncles, and then he would go to jail, my mom would be sad, and I would have ruined the whole family. So, I kept it to myself. I became silent.

I remember one specific beating. I came home late from school. I was in the eleventh grade. I missed the bus and had to walk. My best friend was with me. My father met us at the door. He was drunk and angry and had a brown extension cord in his hand. He made my friend leave. He started whipping me with that cord. I could hear the wind whistling as he violently brought the cord down. I listened to the sound of the contact against my clothing, but I felt nothing. I did not move. I did not scream, and I refused to cry. I was so angry at this unjust, unwarranted act that I just stood there staring at him with hatred in my eyes. In his drunken stupor, it took him a while to notice he was not getting the desired reaction. Eventually, he peered into my cold, hollow eyes. One hot tear rolled down my cheek. He backed away. We did not speak again until nearly twenty years later. Again, I was mute.

I became more withdrawn and depressed. I lost my voice, and the ability to speak for the little girl inside that was crying for love and attention. The little girl wanted to be seen and protected. I lost my ability to feel and connect. Refusing to cry shut down a part of me. I became cold and distant. The molestation I experienced robbed me of my self-esteem and worth. Because I thought so little of myself at this point, I allowed other men to take advantage of me. I did not know who I was and did not understand that I had value.

You may have never lived with the pain of depression brought on by trauma, but your hurt may hurt just the same. My crisis has taught me to recognize others in pain and has given me the desire to help others walk out of their place of pain. We are not what has happened to us, but we can use the pressure of that pain to produce something beautiful. Something that will bring not only healing and joy to us but to everyone around us. Hurting people hurt people. I know what pain looks like. I feel others' pain. When they do not know what to ask for, I can be that hand to reach down to pull them out of their sunken place into the sunshine to live.

My crisis championed a cry in me that says, "I have experienced enough pain that I don't ever want anyone to feel what I felt." It has taught me to be gracious and patient with myself and others. No one wants to experience pain, but nothing can replace the effect that the pressure of pain has on producing something beautiful.

Everyday life gets just a little brighter, and when my old friend comes knocking, I start singing the old song from Rose Royce, "Love Don't Live Here Anymore."

My crisis EMPOWERED me to bring others out of their place of pain.

Jeanette Corprew-Cox is an entrepreneur, author of several children's books, retired elementary school educator of thirty-five years, and proud Proprietor of Just Creative with Imaginary Friends and Company, where she brings life to her twin characters, Sparkle and Glitter. Through her company, she empowers young children to value themselves, develop good character traits, and grow their imaginations. Jeanette was born and raised in Chesapeake, VA, with her twin sister Annette and nine other siblings. Their parents taught them the importance of displaying character traits and being respectful. As Jeanette grew older, she realized she had a love for expanding the minds of children. During her collaboration with parents and children, it was revealed that there was a significant deficit in children showing high self-esteem, respect for others, and the ability to explore their imaginations. Jeanette's passion led her in a new and exciting direction, using her gifts to bless those children.

Connect with Jeanette at www.sparkle-glitter.com

CRISIS 7

Grief Propelled Me to My "NEXT"

Jeanette Corprew-Cox

The unexpected death of my twin sister and best friend, Annette, is the very contradiction of "For God is not unrighteous to forget your work and labor of love, which ye has shewed toward His Name, in that you have ministered to the saints and do minister," (Hebrews 6:10). She had committed her life and heart to the ministry and served with a spirit of excellence, so why did God allow Annette to die?

She was the epitome of Hebrews 6:10. She was a warm-hearted servant who tirelessly served God's people and her leaders so her death made me feel God had forgotten her labor of love, servitude, and heart toward His people. I trusted God, but I felt He let me down when Annette died. My faith was in God, but when she passed, my confidence was shattered. I was so angry. I was so disappointed. I was in such distress that I even said to God, "You could have taken someone other than my twin." I even had suggestions of people, He could have taken, including some of my family members. She was such a giving person. Annette would help in any way she could. I did not see any good in Him allowing her to die. This was a crisis that I thought I would never live through or see become a blessing in my life.

April 2011 was a hectic month in our church and her ministry. It was the month we celebrated the pastor's and church's anniversary. She was preparing to go out of town to Chesapeake, Virginia, to attend a homegoing service for a friend of the family. However, she wanted to complete some ministry responsibilities before leaving. That's just the type of person she was. She always wanted to help others first. Annette put everyone before herself. Before she got on the road, I was expecting her to call me. It was not uncommon that we would talk three or four times a day. As the hours passed, I was worried that I had not heard from her. I continued to call her, but there was no response. Her phone went directly to her voicemail. It was not until the crisis unfolded that I found out that her phone battery was low and eventually died.

Finally, my phone rang. Imagine the disappointment because it was not Annette. It was one of my older sisters. In an anxious, excited, and concerned voice, she told me Annette was taken to the hospital. During the homegoing service, Annette got up from her seat and told my sister she did not feel well. Suddenly, Annette collapsed, and my sister caught her in her arms. Someone called 911; paramedics arrived within five minutes.

They gathered information from my eldest sister, stabilized Annette, and transported her to the hospital. Doctors ran several tests, but Annette never regained consciousness. The doctors met with the family to share the despairing results that there was nothing else they could do. They airlifted her to a more equipped hospital, where another series of tests revealed that my dear sister was bleeding on the brain. My sister remains on the ventilator for another two weeks. We knew we would have to make a difficult decision. Why God? How could this be happening? I felt lonely, abandoned, and hopeless without my dear friend.

Annette had not even passed, but I began to feel the weight of grief. I asked God, "Why am I going through this turmoil?" I constantly kept asking God why. Why do I have to bear all this pain? I sat in a state of disbelief. I thought about what David said in Psalms 25:18, "Lord, look upon my affliction and my pain; and forgive all my sins." I was afflicted by my own emotions. This condition was disastrous. Again, why her? She was such an anointed and skillful helper to the Kingdom of God. I cannot tell you how many prayers I prayed. Tears rolled down my face like a waterfall. I felt helpless.

It was time for a family meeting. We had faith in God, but our faith was shattered because of the circumstances. We went on a fast and asked that God's will be done in this matter.

I continued to ask Him why. Annette was a diligent worker and spent more time at church than anyone else I knew. She was a faithful and committed steward. When I pondered on that scripture about God not forgetting your labor of love, it certainly gave me some hope that everything would be all right. This was a battle, and I needed Him to intervene. Romans 8:31 stayed in my heart, "If God be for me, who can be against me?" I knew Him to be a God that would fight your battles. I needed Him to do just that. We continued to fast and pray. How would we know God's perfect will in this? We needed a miracle. I continued to believe Isaiah 53:5 (NKJV):

> "But He was wounded for our transgressions, He was bruised for our iniquities; the chastisement for our peace was upon Him, and by His stripes, we are healed."

What plans did God have in store for Annette? I was not ready to be without my sister. We had so many beautiful memories to share. How would we tell our story? We talked about writing about our experiences. I wondered if it would happen. My mom was in the room when I decided to glance at Annette. To my surprise, she smiled at me. Suddenly, I called out to my mom, "Look, Mom! She just smiled." That encouraged my heart!

Many days passed without progress. The fourteenth day had come. Our family had a decision to make. It was time to put all our faith in Jesus. I still believed she would come through this. Our family decided to pull the plug on the life support and ventilator. She was moved to another room.

The wait was still on. I contemplated going home to Maryland. It was the hardest decision I have ever made. I decided to drive back to Maryland since there was no change in her condition. I was still angry with God. I continued to wipe tear after tear.

Two more days went by. My phone rang on a Tuesday evening. It was not the call I was ready to receive. "She didn't make it!" The voice said at the other end. I literally screamed to the top of my lungs, ran into my bedroom, and laid down. I sobbed. The tears just would not stop. Was this really happening? This cannot be true. But Lord, "I thought you said you took all those stripes for our healing." "Lord, why her?" "You could have taken anybody else, but why Annette?" "She was so giving and loving." There was not a thing she would not do for you. This pain was deep and crushed me to the point I was numb. I refused to understand the outcome. They tell me that God does not make any mistakes. How could this not be a mistake?

Thoughts of regret began to swallow my thoughts. There was one in particular. I never got a chance to finish writing that book about us. I had started writing it, but my computer crashed and the whole story was gone. Now she is gone!

We prepared to lay Annette to rest. We had the homegoing celebration and so many people attended to demonstrate their love for Annette. They came from near and far. The service was exactly as I visualized it. It was undoubtedly a celebration of her life, but it did not help me with my grief. I could not handle the deep depression I had fallen into. Days and days passed, and I did not get better. I asked God to deliver me and show me what was next for my life if Annette was not there.

Suddenly, God showed up for me. You would not believe what happened one day! Waking up from a long, peaceful night's sleep, I rolled over. When God visited me, it was like sadness and selfishness vanished. What came to my mind was absolutely amazing! I said to myself, "God has a way that is mighty sweet." It was like a burden was lifted off my shoulders. The hurt disappeared. I felt happy again. The Lord let me know there was a solution to my hurt. I walked into my living room and sat in one of my favorite chairs. I reclined the brown suede chair as far back as I could. Then I heard a still, soft voice. Was I really hearing what I thought I heard? The Lord said unto me, "Finish your book."

"Are you telling me to finish the book I promised Annette I would write?" I asked. "Positive thoughts overcame my negative thoughts." I pondered them repeatedly. Was God telling me to author the book I started to write several years ago?

Did I want to start writing the book again? It had been well over ten years. I thought about keeping my word. I have always been a person who knew keeping your word was more important than anything. Matthew 22:37-40 says, "So, if we ought to love our neighbor, we should keep our word to them."

My parents taught us that keeping your word was part of your character. People trust you when you keep your word. That thought kept resurfacing in my mind. Even though Annette was no longer with us, I knew what I said. "Jeanette, sit down and make it happen!" It was time to get over it! It was time to forget about losing the entire story on the computer and ask God to help me. I did not know where to start. He said, "You take the first step, and I will do the rest."

I had the idea for an ABC book to tell our story so I did what God told me to do. I took the first step and began to write. I spent a short amount of time developing the story because I had already begun writing it more than ten years ago. I also knew that God was with me and gave me the ability to finish the story. I felt accomplished, and I surprised myself.

After completing the book, the Lord led me to a publisher who did an extraordinary job publishing my first literary work.

My book, *The ABC's In the Days of My Life as a Twin*, won a literary award in 2020.

After receiving this honor, God brought to my remembrance my professional teaching career for which I retired from after thirty-five years. He reminded me that He had gifted me with the ability of creativity and this gift was immensely helpful, encouraging and brought laughter, fun and healing to many students. I believe God was saying, "Your gift can also bring healing to your anger, hurt and loneliness that comes from the passing of Annette." God helped me to see I could us my imagination to not only be healed but to pretend that Annette would always be with me.

God gave me the name of my business, allowing me to continue my sister's legacy. That is how Just Creative with Imaginary Friends and Company all started. I wanted the initials in my name to be part of my business name.

I always enjoyed dressing up like characters, so I created characters who would represent Annette and me. In that way, I could continue to tell our story. First, the Lord gave me an idea to create a life-sized doll that looked like me. I shared my idea with a friend in North Carolina, and she told me just what to do. Because of her gifted abilities, I now have Glitter, who became my imaginary friend, Annette. Who do you think that life-sized doll became? Oh yes! She became my twin sister. I named her Glitter, and I am Sparkle. There you have it!

Using my imagination, Annette would always be near me. Whenever I read my books about Annette, it is as if she is right there. God is a sweet and awesome God! I thought Annette's death would take me out but look at God! Not only have I published two books, but He has allowed me to write three books, with more on the way. I get joy when I think about the many things we did as twins. What better way to preserve those precious memories than through a storybook!

After authoring that book, the Lord gave me another idea for a book, which included Annette and me. *Sparkle and Glitter Show Character* is about a set of adventurous twins who embark on an incredible journey full of memorable quests and life-long character traits they learned as they grew up. The third book, *The Adventures of Homeschooling with Sparkle and Glitter,* finds twins navigating homeschool life during the COVID-19 Pandemic. I am still amazed with how God orchestrated my sister's death to show me how I could keep her alive and use my gifts.

What I thought was a curse turned out to be a blessing. Just Creative with Imaginary Friends and Company were birthed, and I became the author of three children's books.

My crisis EMPOWERED me to become an entrepreneur and a children's book author.

Acquanett Jones Chance is a minister and mentor. Her passion is singing, and she has a heart for serving others. A native of Danville, VA, she is a partner at Compassion Danville, where she serves as a member of the leadership and worship teams. As an aspiring women's ministry executive, she acknowledges herself as a woman of valor who believes wholeheartedly through her testimony. Isaiah 61:1 says, "He heals the brokenhearted and binds up their wounds." She desires to encourage others to strive to live free from bondage by being healthy and whole. She is a casework counselor and received her Bachelor of Arts degree in Sociology from St. Augustine's University. She is currently attending Regent University pursuing her Master's degree in Counseling. Acquanett is a divorced mother of four adult children, Taylor, Justin, Kayla, and Jade, and two granddaughters, Kennedy, and Destiny.

Connect with Acquanett at Mrsachance1@gmail.com

CRISIS 8

Timing is Everything

Acquanett Jones Chance

He said if I talked, I would regret it. A few weeks prior, I received a phone call from her saying, "We need this to stay quiet." Unbelievable! How desperate could they be? I paused for a second in disbelief. I could not believe she was bold enough to call me, but I was not moved. After a moment, I asked her to repeat what she said, and she did. She even used a pleasant tone. How nice of her.

Maybe she thought if her words were kind enough, I would gracefully bow down and comply. Then we could all get back to life as we knew it. We worshipped in the same sanctuary on Sunday mornings as if all were well. They would find solace in believing I would never say a word. Do not get me wrong, there were some choice words I could have used, but what good would that have done? In the words of our former First Lady Michelle Obama, "When they go low, we go high." Going high does not exempt you from pain or feeling your emotions. However, your response should reflect the result of the problem, and the problem was not going to end with me. After all, I was her

First Lady. Although I was filled with pain and emotions, this was their mess, not mine. I would continue to be the lady I was known to be, all while keeping silent.

Keeping quiet became my Achilles heel. Although it was my choice not to speak on the matter, I always believed that putting pen to paper and sharing the thoughts behind my journey could help someone else and free me from the very thing that held me captive and prevented me from being healthy and whole. I am sure it appeared as though I had it all together on the outside, but I was falling apart on the inside. The silence was my crisis.

Silence had a stronghold on me. It became the heavyweight champion of my life. It weighed me down and seemed as if it would never lift. You see, I chose silence; it did not choose me. I could have talked long ago, but what would I have gained? Who would have listened to me? What would I have said? Silence became a part of my wardrobe, and I wore it like a coat. It seemed to fit so well. It helped to cover all our failures and all my fears.

Wondering what I feared the most! Well, I feared the same thing so many others feared. I feared what we would look like in the sight of others and what they would think or say. I also feared facing my reality. Who wants anyone to know their family is functioning dysfunctionally? You see, people often ask, "How is the family?" The response was always the same;

"We are all hanging in there." So, to keep it simple, I kept it quiet. But in my silence, I realized I had some pride issues I needed to deal with.

All this manifested over time after being in a very unhealthy marriage. I was married for twenty-six years, but the last eight years were filled with treacherous events that tore my spirit and contributed to our divorce. The marriage had been falling apart for quite some time before it slowly faded. Although my husband and I had our struggles, they were our struggles, and when we failed, they were our failures.

Do not get me wrong; we also had some wins. But as I look back over our lives, I realize we never celebrated those wins, big or small. People probably cheered for us more than we cheered for ourselves. Being a pastor and a pastor's wife comes with challenges that other marriages may never face. Who we were and our responsibility made the attack on the marriage much greater and gave me even more reason to keep things quiet. The marriage was far from perfect, but I was determined to hang in there until I realized it was no longer just the two of us. There were three.

We had our children, our church, and a plus one. We were rocky before she came along. We were hanging on by threads. I often prayed, believing God would heal what was broken and restore our marriage. My husband and I had many talks that ended well, so the marriage ending was unforeseen to me. Divorce was not in my plans, and I was determined to make sure my children did not have the same experience I had as a child of divorced parents.

All of this was painful. I cried many nights and shed silent tears for many years. But I knew things would change, and God would turn it around. So, in the sanctuary, I kept worshiping and praising God as they continued to be who they were to each other. I have no idea how they did it, but they kept it moving.

Honestly, they thought I was following through with their request to stay quiet. It was working in their favor because they did not hear a peep from me. They failed to realize that I did not have to say a word. "For there is nothing hidden that will not be revealed," Luke 8:17. This should have been their greatest worry, not mine. I never came up against them—not once. God would not let it be so. I am reminded, "There is a time to be silent and speak," (Ecclesiastes 3:7). There was no need for a publicity show.

On Friday, August 1, 2014, he made a comment that stuck with me. I had gained access to his phone without his knowledge, and I sent a text message to her saying, "I miss you." She had no idea it was me. She replied using the exact words. I approached him and said, "I know everything. I just gave her a call." He had no clue. I confronted him, and he confessed. I told him to call her to let her know I was aware, and he did. "Hey, Roller found out about us," he said. Roller? Really? Ok. If that was their joke, then Holy Roller, I will be. I may have been at the center of their jokes, but my relationship with God is not funny to me. And it is just that—*my* relationship. I am grateful for it. Had it not been for God, I could have lost my mind behind this stupidity, but He helped me to keep it together.

One thing was for sure, God had seen it all—even my arrest brought about by foolishness concerning the two of them. I questioned a hotel receipt yet again. This caused an argument, during which I grabbed his lips to stop him from yelling. He left and contacted the police. Can you believe my acrylic nail was broken, and it split his lip? The police arrived at 2 a.m., questioned me about an assault, handcuffed me in front of my children, and placed me under arrest. Talk about shame.

Now you see why I stayed quiet. It was not because I feared them. It was because of the embarrassment. Here we are, church leaders, and the First Lady has been arrested. How is that for a headline? But the plot thickens. I felt like our family was really under attack. It seemed the more I prayed, the worse it became. I was living in silence and shame, but they kept it moving.

The turmoil did not stop there. Just four months later, he told me he was heading to Richmond, VA, to attend worship service and would stay overnight. I was no fool. By this time, it made me no never mind. God was about to reveal it all. An ATM withdrawal at a hotel showed up on my bank statement. The address was included, so I decided to leave Chesapeake, VA, and take a trip. I knew what I would find when I got there. I was not going to stir up anything. I only needed to show my face so the lies could end. I was not even nervous. I was just tired. I got there, and the timing was perfect. As I arrived that night, he called my cell phone while walking into the hotel. I was pulling into the parking lot, and he had no idea I was looking right at him. He said, "My phone is dying, and I left my charger at home. I will call you in the morning." These are some conversations I will never forget. After he walked in, I made my way to the desk and showed that I had the same last name as him to get the room number. I sat in the hallway for a few moments, trying to decide what to do. I did not want to wait too long.

Unfortunately, my plan did not work too well. I knocked on the door and tried to push my way in. I stuck my hand in the doorway, and she banged the door constantly on my finger. It bled, and my college class ring was damaged. That ring was a gift from my father that I still wear today. That night did not end so well. He left, and she stayed behind. I was not leaving until she left. She finally walked out, and I followed her. The First Lady wanted to push her down the stairs, but her saving grace was my arrest from four months prior that I had not yet gone to court for. What they both failed to realize is that life is serious. People are sleeping in their graves behind the very act that occurred at that hotel. I thank God for keeping my mind. I could have snapped quicker than a blink. I believe it could have happened.

And I still remained silent! I pressed charges, and he asked me to drop them, so I did. I did not want the publicity for the church nor to shame my children. They were tired and wanted out, and so did I. I felt stuck, and this was a revelation to me that God was not going to do anything. He had shown me everything, and I decided to walk away from it all.

The pandemic showed up, and I had been contemplating my moves. I wanted to make sure my youngest child had finished high school. My children suffered in ways you would never believe. The stress and duress were unbearable at times. I talked to a pastor who was a close friend to us both.

"Why do you think I stayed?" I asked.

"You are a woman of faith, and you believe in family," he said. I had nothing left, but I was reminded that God was my everything.

This is my story. I could never have been convinced that this would be. I embraced my fears and my failures. I have found my voice. I am no longer ashamed. I gave my all. I was not perfect. I did not deserve it, but God allowed it. Life is what it will be, and it does not take God by surprise. I am thankful for everything I have endured. I have embraced my struggles, and it made me stronger. I am a Warrior, and God worked it out for my good.

I did not curse my crisis by speaking at the wrong time. I could have spoken out of anger and bitterness, which could have turned out to be a disaster, all because I was not ready to embrace the emotions that would come with it. I am reminded of Ecclesiastes 3:3, "There is a time and a season under the heavens for all things." I believe now is my time. The process was not easy, but I have forgiven them!

My crisis EMPOWERED me to forgive and become VICTORIOUS!

Jackie Grice is the CEO of J Diamond Inc., a multimillion-dollar transportation company. Her passion as an innovator drove her to pursue a Mechanical Engineering degree from The University of Virginia. Her desire to serve her community led her to start her non-profit, Create Vision, in 2017. Her passion for small businesses and people led her to begin Launching Deeper Enterprises, a business and personal development coaching, consulting, and strategy company. Launching Deeper Enterprises, LLC helps people discover their purpose to create the business and life they dreamed of using her L5 acceleration, Pursue Purpose and Prosper business program. Jackie is most known for her Masterclass series, The Blueprint to Launching

Deeper, where she sits down with the world's most influential Leaders of this age. Jackie is most proud of being the wife of Wayne and the mother of Diamond and Wayne Grice II.

Connect with Jackie at www.launchingdeeper.com

CRISIS 9

Launch Deeper

Jacqueline Grice

I drove away from my house in tears. A place where I should have felt the most secure had turned into a place of despair and regret. I had no idea that a simple prayer and declaration I had made months earlier would lead me to a place I had not been to for over thirty years. How did I even get here? How did I return to a place that had become foreign and unfamiliar? A place I swore I would never return. A place where I felt alone and hopeless?

Thirty years prior, I suffered from depression. No one talked about being depressed when I was younger. In my world, depression was not something you shared with people; you kept it to yourself. Even if you did share what you were feeling, no one knew about depression in my small community or that those feelings were signs of a mental illness. I remember my mother saying that I was melancholy. To me, the word "melancholy" seemed normal. It did not seem at all serious. Years later, I realized that being "melancholy" and depressed were two different things. Back then, I felt sad and lonely at times. I just thought that whatever melancholy meant to a teenage girl wasn't that serious because those feelings did not prevent me from excelling socially or academically in high school.

When I went away to college, those same "melancholy" feelings showed up differently. I found myself unable to get out of bed in the mornings. I struggled with getting to class. I constantly felt inadequate, as though I had let people down — like my life was worthless and everyone around me would be much better off if I were out of the picture. I felt I wasn't living up to the expectations of others. I felt like a failure, and the sadness that I dubbed as melancholy had manifested into something more profound, and I couldn't pull myself out of this dark empty state. I felt overwhelmed, and I couldn't figure out why. Where were these thoughts coming from? I even begin to question the value of my life.

I started thinking that I was flawed and that this would be my life. I remember finding scriptures in the Bible that supported this thinking. Somehow, I was cursed. I did not understand that depression was the root cause, not my inadequacies. I did not know what I had done to feel this way, but I had convinced myself that I would never escape these feelings. I had decided that I was just that person the Bible spoke about — the one whom God cursed. There was a stronghold, and I could not see the truth of God's word. I could only see what the enemy wanted me to see — that I was better off dead. Somehow, I convinced myself that my parents, who loved me more than life itself, and my siblings, who cared for me dearly, would somehow be relieved if I were no longer in this world.

It did not matter that I was a student at a prestigious university. It did not matter that I was once at the top of my class with a promising future. All I knew was that I did not want to get up. I did not want to go to my classes. I did not want to exist in pain. I felt I was falling deeper into this dark place, and I could not pull myself out of this horrible pit. Even with all the great victories I had experienced, I had convinced myself that, ultimately, I would fail. A dark hole was waiting; a pit was waiting behind every open door. There would be a trap somewhere down the path. Even though good things would happen in my life, it would only be a matter of time before something dreadful would follow. I continued to convince myself of this fate and constantly looked for evidence to support the lies I started to believe about my life and future. So, I decided to spare myself and those around me the disappointment of being a failure. One day, I decided I would end it all.

Fortunately, God's plans for my life were greater than the plan I had to end my life. God saved me! As I sat in the still of the night, in a dark car alone in a park in Virginia, God intervened and saved my life!

Looking back at that way of thinking, I cannot understand how I even thought that way. But back then, I did. And as I fast-forwarded thirty years into the present while driving away from my home, those feelings of hopelessness and desperation that I thought were long gone had resurfaced.

Months before that desperate drive from my house, I went to Dubai with my family and friends to celebrate the New Year of 2020. When I returned, I was amazed by what I had seen. I asked God "to take me where my feet could not take me." I wanted God to take my ordinary life and transform it into the life I had only imagined. I saw greatness in Dubai and wanted God to use me for His greater plan and purpose. Again, at the time, I did not understand the magnitude of the prayer. A few months after saying that prayer almost daily, the COVID-19 pandemic hit the world.

My husband and I are in the transportation industry, and the pandemic devastated our business. The pressure of customers demanding hundreds of thousands of dollars of non-refundable deposits back became overwhelming, as well as the pressures of working with my spouse. It wasn't like we had different careers. This thing called COVID was affecting us both at the same time. The fact that we were both experiencing something we had never experienced before was devastating to our marriage.

We had always thrived, and our business was always successful. Even when we started years ago, we were successful in our own right. As CEO and co-owner, this was the first time I did not know what to do to save our company. I prided myself on being innovative and operating with keen business acumen. I had cutting-edge ideas but could not think of how they could save our type of business. All the ideas I tried to implement seemed to fail. Doors closed one after the other. All the proposals I thought would help us pivot were rejected one after the other.

I knew the government was offering assistance to small businesses, so I went after everything I could. One after the other, my applications got lost in the system. Multiple system glitches impacted my loan and grant processing. With each call for assistance, the resolution seemed further and further away. At one point, the government stated that we had not suffered a loss even after showing we were down over 75% in revenue. It was a never-ending nightmare.

Almost daily my husband and I were at odds. We both blamed one another and said, "We should have done this; we should have done that. Why didn't you do this? Why didn't you do that?" It was a constant battle of blame. I oversaw our company's finances and business development, so it all seemed to fall on my shoulders.

My husband, who had looked to me for the solutions and answers in the past, saw the same person who had managed multiple millions of dollars in assets completely freeze. In a world where all you heard was the word "pivot," I could not move. I was paralyzed by fear. There were stories of people who owned breweries and restaurants that were shut down, so they began making masks or hand sanitizers. I was mentally stuck! I could not see that we had anything that could be used for manufacturing another good or service. I remember crying to God, saying, "Why did we choose this business? This business is cursed." Those words were an echo from thirty years ago. Those old voices I thought were gone said, "See, you were doing good. You thought you were achieving something. You thought you and your husband were progressing, but remember, you always fail."

I found myself asking those same questions I asked myself thirty years ago. Why am I even here? Why am I such a failure? That lie started getting louder. "You're cursed. All the paperwork you put in and all the efforts to get your business and marriage out of the shape it was in are failing, and it's all your fault because, ultimately, you're cursed."

During the years leading up to COVID, my husband and I had connected with some other couples and grew remarkably close — at least, I thought. Even those friendships ended in ways I could never have imagined, and again, I took all the blame. Again, I sat there and said, "It's all your fault because you're cursed." It seemed as though God was stripping away everything I thought I needed. Everything I thought mattered. Everything!

The day I drove away from my house in tears was so clear. I got in my car to get as far away from my home as possible. I needed some relief from the constant barrage of being blamed for everything. My husband was under a tremendous amount of pressure as well. As a man, it was hard to imagine losing everything and wondering how we got here. So unfortunately, he blamed me for the business and the friendships failing. I was desperate to hear from God, but all I heard was, "You're cursed, and you may as well die."

I parked the car and cried and cried because I felt I had no one. I cried because I thought I was cursed. I cried because I could not believe those thoughts had resurfaced after all these years. But unlike last time, the love of my two children and the love of God enveloped me. As hard as the enemy was trying to pull me backward, the Holy Spirit was drawing me closer to God.

I turned my car around and drove home. The issue was still facing me, and my husband was still angry at me. The bills were still coming in, and the solutions were as cloudy as ever. Even though I was at my breaking point, I knew God had a great plan for my life. I knew the enemy would not be after me this hard if I were not supposed to make an impact in this world. As hopeless as I felt, I knew my children needed me, and my husband loved me underneath all the hurt. I knew I could never do that to my family again.

Desperate to hear what God was trying to tell me, I reached out to my pastor. He always said he had a good ear, and I knew that to be true. Since I could not hear God, I prayed he could. I knew God was trying to tell me something, but I was so busy begging God to get me out of this awful crisis that I neglected to sit quietly to hear Him. After the phone call with my pastor, he instructed me to spend two days in silence, shutting off the phone and all conversations. He advised me to ask God two questions. The first question was, "Lord, what am I to pursue?" And the second was, "What is the strategy in that pursuit?"

Coincidentally, the next day, the day he instructed me to start, was a virtual silent session with a group in Richmond, Virginia. I knew God was up to something. I was eager for the session to start. So, that Tuesday, I got my journal and pen and sat in a chair under a tree in my front yard. Right away, God started speaking. I could not believe it.

Yes, God started speaking. Oh, my goodness, I had not heard or did not think I had heard Him, but He was speaking all the time. When doors I prayed to open suddenly shut, and things were not going as I thought they should, the friends I thought loved me so much ended up leaving my life; God was speaking. But I could not hear Him because I was so busy trying to figure it out myself. I was so busy trying to keep things and people in my life that weren't supposed to be there anymore.

I was so busy expecting God to give me solutions to save these failed friendships. I wanted God to tell me how to fix my marriage and keep my business. I was seeking a one-and-done financial plan to escape our situation, but God was not speaking that language. God was answering a prayer, a declaration that hit me at the beginning of the year. I said to God, "Lord, take me where my feet can't take me." God said, "That's what I'm doing. I am answering your prayer. When you prayed that prayer, you wanted something so drastic and amazing to happen in your life that you said, 'God, take me where my feet, where my physical capabilities can't take me.'" So, God was speaking to me and saying, "If I take you where you can't go, where your friends can't take you, where your finances can't take you, then I have to remove all those things you have relied on in your past."

It hit me that God was shutting doors to get me where I needed to go. In silence, I heard God speak. He had to get me to a breaking point in my crisis where I was so desperate that I would seek His voice only and not my voice or the voices of my friends — not my will, but God's will. I was so desperate that I was willing to shut down everything to hear God speak to me. In the middle of chaos, in the middle of my life being turned upside down; in the middle of my marriage being on the brink of divorce; in the middle of feeling betrayed, lonely, and rejected; in the middle of a pandemic; and in the middle of darkness, God was speaking.

And the crazy thing is that God told me to launch deeper in Him in the middle of my most painful season. He told me there was a blessing in the middle of this crisis. He told me to launch deeper and that there was something greater for me if I trusted Him to take me where my feet could not.

"Okay," I replied. "But what does that even mean, God?" God revealed that what I thought was a great business, great friendships, and financial security was just surface-level stuff. He had more extraordinary plans for me — more incredible and significant innovations for my business. There were deep, loving, and genuine relationships that were waiting for me. And God revealed that what He had in mind for my marriage was so much more than the marriage I had known for the last twenty years.

God said to launch deeper. He said, "Don't be afraid; I need you to cast your net — again."

I thought about the scripture with Simon Peter (Luke 5:4-11). When Jesus stepped on Simon's boat, He told Simon to launch out into the deep, and Simon, even though he knew this was not the right time to catch fish and after a day of failure, was obedient enough to listen to God and go back out and cast his nets again. And that is what God was telling me. God was saying, "You know what, Jackie? I need you to go back out. I know the banks are not calling you. I know you feel you do not have any friends. I know you feel your marriage has failed. I know you feel like a failure. I know you feel you have been unable to be innovative and creative and develop strategies to save your business, but Jackie, I want you to cast your net out into deep water."

God told me that what He had for me was so excellent and profound that He needed me to go beyond where I ever thought I could go. God wanted me to go beyond my limiting beliefs, beyond what I thought I could do, beyond barriers I never thought I could break, and beyond my understanding that I could have a marriage, I only dreamed of having. He told me I could have people around me who loved me — people who genuinely loved me for who I was, flaws and all.

"And when you do this," God said, "I want you to show others how to do it, too. I want you to be an example of how you operate in a crisis, a pandemic, a recession, a shutdown, and a drought. I want you to teach others how to launch out into the deep no matter the situation because I speak loudest in the middle of chaos. In the middle of a crisis, I do not want you to shut down, be fearful, or look at other people's situations. Instead, throw your net out as deep as it will go. That is what I want you to do. That is where I need you to go."

Truthfully, it is easy to shut down when chaos comes. It is easy to revert to old habits and old ways of thinking. Blaming others in the middle of a crisis is what keeps you stuck. That is where the enemy wants us to go. He does not want us to push past the crisis because victory is on the other side. There's victory on the other side of what we thought was a failure. Understanding how not to curse your crisis is deep-water thinking, but in deep water are great things — big things. In deep water are limitless possibilities and a life with the purpose He has called each of us to live. Launch deeper, never stop, and most importantly, don't curse your crisis because God wants to use it for His glory.

My crisis EMPOWERED
me to launch deeper.

CRISIS 10

Lady Tina Olds is the daughter of the Late Rev. Francis and Lady Barbara Askew. She is married to Superintendent Anthony M. Olds, Sr, and the proud mother of four children, Anthony Jr. (Simone), Joy, Thomas, and T'Nia. She recently launched, When Women Pray (WWP), a prayer ministry designed to intercede and encourage women of all ages. She is the First Lady of Intercessory Prayer Ministries COGIC and mentors young men and women. She attended Tidewater Community College and Norfolk State University and is presently attending Regent University, all in Virginia. She is a Human Resources Associate with Virginia Beach City Public Schools, employed for twenty-eight years. Tina stands firm in

Jeremiah 29:11, "For I know the plans I have for you, "declares the Lord," plans to prosper you and not to harm you, plans to give you hope and a future.

Connect with Tina at tolds5262@gmail.com

From Riches to Rags

Tina Olds

Have you ever had a mountain top experience? Everything is going well. You are unstoppable. Nothing can hold you back. Your relationship with God is one hundred. Your relationship with your brand-new husband is magnificent and ready to SOAR. Nothing can go wrong!

Have you ever had a desert valley experience? You feel parched, exhausted, and helpless. One of the many crises I have experienced made me feel like a desert valley. I felt my bottom had been entirely snatched from under me, and I was left to die. I felt ashamed, worthless, and embarrassed; I wanted to crawl under a dry cactus in that desert and die. Did I compromise my marriage, integrity, and mental capability for what I had done? How could I explain this stupid act that I had committed?

On February 23, 1991, I married the man of my dreams. In front of hundreds of witnesses, we vowed to be together for better or worse, for richer, for poorer, in sickness and health, and to love and to cherish till death do us part. We were that jolly couple that was deeply in love.

I worked at the bank, and he was the minister of music at church. Some days when he was not busy at work, he would come to my job with a car full of senior citizens. It did not bother me because we were in love, and he worked for the church. Life was grand. Our marriage was at an all-time high! All the bills were paid, and we were living life. My banking job and his church job were getting us through.

I was advancing in the banking field, and everything was swell. One day while working at the bank, my friend had an emergency and needed me to cash an extensive check for her. She was a bank member, so I expected everything to be fine. It was after 2 p.m., and we knew we had time to deposit the money into her account by the following day.

No, I did not steal the money, but the moment to make the deposit the following day never came. Returned checks came in at 10:00 a.m. I was a little nervous because my friend had yet to make a deposit or call. Soon after, I realized things were not aligned, and the desert valley experience began.

The branch manager called me into the office and asked several questions concerning the transaction I had made the day before. Even though my supervisor knew I was a Christian and would never steal from the company, I had broken the company's policy. One can only imagine the thoughts that were going through my head. I questioned my integrity and wondered if this had happened to me. I had only been married a few months. What would my husband say? Did I compromise my life for this friend? My emotions raced. I cried and begged for mercy. Then I had to call my husband.

I had to explain to my sweet husband that I had just been dismissed from my job and needed to be picked up. The walk from the bank's front door to our car was a walk of shame. Tears flowed, and I felt I would be sick to my stomach. Trying to explain this situation to my new husband was very arduous. He wanted answers that I did not have. He was vexed with my friend, and I felt as if he would leave me. I knew he would not leave me forever, but he needed time to process everything.

I trusted someone with a need, and she did what she needed to improve her situation. Even though her intentions were good, the plan failed, leaving me with a distraught husband and no job. Thank God for praying in-laws. His family rushed to our aid. They immediately came to our little apartment and began to pray. I was thankful for the prayers, but my insides felt like someone had snatched my heart out and left me for dead. Of course, no one knew how I felt but God and me. I was disgusted with myself. Without being saved and filled with the Holy Ghost, the club or ABC store would have been my best friend that night. I wanted to get rid of the embarrassment. The devil was whipping my tail.

Even though I felt my life was ending and I had made the biggest mistake, God had a word for me. Our family is a family that believes in prophecy. When the Spirit speaks, you can take it to the bank that it is coming to pass. Will I stand firm on what the Spirit says, or will I have a pity party and sink into my feelings? The Spirit said, "This was all meant to happen." What! I was out of a job, and this was meant to happen. I had a real problem with this answer, but I accepted God's will. I asked God many times why He allowed this to happen to me. Was I cursed for the sins of my youth? Did I not obey God when He instructed me to say or do something? These are the questions Christians ask themselves when tests and trials happen. Did I forget about the vows I made when I asked God to help me in previous situations, and He did? I needed to stretch my faith.

The next day I visited my parents' houses. My father must have been the calmest man I have ever known. God bless his soul, and may he rest in peace. He never said much and was full of wisdom. When he found out about my catastrophe, he asked me to come home for a visit. Of course, I was so upset and ashamed of what I had done. With my husband by my side, I told my father what had happened. Something about talking to your father causes your emotions to be uncontrollable. All my baby girl habits kicked in. I was a total wreck. After explaining all the details, I told him who the person was. He calmly asked, "Now, what are you going to do?"

That was the last thing on my mind. I was unemployed. My husband was a minister of music. My job at the bank provided all our health and life insurance. Dad was a man of few words, but his words always had volume. He always said, "Don't get so emotional." This may have been because he lived in the house with six women. He encouraged me not to get emotional and asked if I could forgive the person. After deep meditation, I said, "Yes." His final words before he sent me and my husband home were, **"Don't stir in the stink."** This statement means that if you forgive someone for what they have done, then do not talk about it to everyone. His philosophy is that the more you stir in the stink, the stinker it will get, and it can make someone look bad and kill their reputation.

When I arrived at my mom's house, three of my sisters were waiting by the door to hear the details. My sisters, who were not there, were waiting to receive a phone call from me. I agreed to stop stirring, and my husband and I went home.

My friend, whom I sacrificed my entire career for, called me and apologized. I knew she felt horrible. I told her that all was well, and I forgave her. I was never angry with her. I may not have been Ms. Bubbly because of the devastation I experienced, but I was never angry. Life can sometimes make you feel like you are in a boxing ring and receiving all the blows. You win some, and you lose some. Well, in this case, I felt as if I was losing.

Life can also put you in some situations where you must make risky decisions. These decisions can put you out there and make you feel as if you were left to die on a desert island. You have nowhere to go and no place to hide. You are just out there all by yourself. At that time in my life that was my definition of life. I found myself going through a state of deep depression, and boy did my heartbreak and ache. I shed many tears. Even though I did not ask, my friend explained the situation. She told me what was supposed to happen that day and what never happened. She explained that the person with good intentions had a setback, and everything fell through a day too late. I was out of a respectable job. As I processed forgiveness and despair, I realized many things. I realized that forgiveness takes time and may not happen overnight. I realized that something had to happen to her to jeopardize my job and our friendship. There must have been some great need for her to do this and know that I would be nice enough to do it. It is called life. Life happens. Because I knew she was living a saved and sanctified life, I knew she did nothing illegal or sinful with the money. Wow, God, all of this was meant to happen.

What took place in my life caused me to reevaluate those marriage vows. I would call this crisis that I experienced, for better or worse. We have experienced other crises, but this had to be the worst. Our economic status began to fade like rose petals being blown away in a tremendous storm. Things began to disappear. We were standing on our faith and trust in God. Living by faith is easy when you are on the top of the mountain, but the desert valley experience is different. Every message I heard in the church seemed like, "Hold on!" How could I hold on after that disaster? My husband was only making $250 a week. That never really bothered us because I had an excellent banking job. My job took care of the significant bills. When I lost my job, we started losing everything. My brand-new Nissan Sentra was repossessed. Our rent started getting behind. However, it was meant to be. That is what the Lord said through grandma Ticky Olds.

Thank God for my husband's gifts of singing and playing the organ and piano. He would accept any appointments outside of his regular schedule. He played for many funeral homes and families he did not know. It still was not enough. Everything was spiraling down. The apartment complex and our proprietor were as patient as they could be. After a while, the eviction notice was on the door. They had to follow their company's policy. Why did those words sound like someone had thrown a brick at my face? We would not have been in this predicament if I had followed the company's policy. Eventually, I found myself at the Virginia Beach Human Services Department. I am not knocking anyone who gets assistance from the state, but this was not my plan. God took us down to the lowest. We still loved each other, and God blessed us with four beautiful, successful children. Once I started having children, all my pride flew out the door. I was the first at the health department to get my WIC checks. The babies had to eat. You could not beat me in the line at the Human Service Department to get my food stamps. Food stamps were like dollar bills, so I could not pretend to be using an EBT card. My pride was flushed down the drain.

One day while pregnant with my oldest, I began to cry uncontrollably. My mom called and asked what was wrong? I told her about my having to use food stamps. Was I expecting sympathy? She explained that it was no longer about me but feeding my children. Mom said, "Girl, get out of your feelings; it's not about you, so get over it." I got up, wiped away my tears, and began to look at life differently. I prioritized my life and realized that if anything were going to get done, I would have to do it. Many other crises have transpired in our lives. We had all our utility bills due at the same time and had to decide as to which was more important. If we paid the electricity bill, the water would be turned off. I would purchase jugs of water so that we could bathe. We have had to uproot our children and move in with family members. So many embarrassing things have taken place in our lives as a Christian family, but it was all meant to happen. Through all of this, I cannot curse the crisis. If God took me through that, He could surely take me through the impossible. Without God and knowing that He had everything in control, I would have definitely been a candidate for a mental institution. God is amazing; He keeps our mind.

Since then, God has called us to ministry. I do not think there have been any crises presented to us that we cannot testify and say, "If He did it for us, then he can do it for you." He is not a respecter of persons (Romans 2:11). Please do not curse your crisis because it was meant to be!

> **My crisis EMPOWERED me to have a heart of forgiveness and patience for what God has for me.**

Latonya Smith is a native of Norfolk, VA, and the youngest of four siblings: two sisters and one brother. She grew up with both parents in the home, and fifty-four years later, they are still committed to one another. She graduated from Booker T. Washington High School in Norfolk, VA, and received an Associate in Social Science from Tidewater Community College. She was a single teenage mother of three, and now they are successful adults; she also has three grandchildren. Latonya has a lifelong career in nursing and has a passion for helping the elderly and people who are still hurting from childhood trauma. She is an advocate for mental health awareness and self-care. She uses her teen pregnancy and life experiences to encourage teenagers and young women to become unique and authentic. She is active in her church and diligent in any task.

Connect with Latonya at Lsmith035@yahoo.com

Come Out of Hiding

Latonya Smith

I was a frantic, immature, lost teenager whose life was about to change forever. Disappointing myself and my parents tormented my mind. Society, church folks, and former associates continuously scrutinized me, leaving me feeling depressed, abandoned, rejected, and in despair. I had no idea what would happen because of this poor choice. It was challenging to manage. As a pregnant teenager, this crisis made me think irrationally and changed the direction of my destiny.

In 1991, at age sixteen, I thought I had met the love of my life. After leaving my high school state championship basketball game, I went to a dance at a hotel in Norfolk, Virginia. When I arrived at the dance, a young man approached me and asked if I would like to dance. I responded, "Yes!" As we danced and talked, we found out we had quite a few things in common. We both enjoyed going to dances and were the youngest in our families. I enjoyed watching basketball, and he played basketball at another local high school. I liked that because I always had to deal with other females who wanted the same guys I wanted and were attracted to the same guys who were attracted to me. This was an unnecessary drama I did not want to experience again. We enjoyed each other's company so much that we exchanged phone numbers that night.

We talked often and enjoyed spending time together. He was the perfect gentleman, and the romance began. We spent more and more time together, and my parents and close friends grew to adore him. I was starry-eyed and in love—so I thought. I thought about him and wanted to be with him all the time. I became truant from school, stayed out late, and then advanced to staying out all night. After a year of dating and practicing this unruly behavior, I became pregnant at seventeen.

I spent my mornings running to the bathroom to vomit, turning the faucet on, and running the fan to drown out the horrible vomiting and grunting sounds as my face nearly touched the water in the toilet. It felt as if the lining of my stomach was producing every spew. I would lay on the floor in the fetal position asking why. I could have had an answer to that question if I had not shut out the one person that could respond, my mother.

Having a prayerful and observant mother, she noticed all the signs and symptoms of my pregnancy. Whom was I trying to fool anyway? It certainly was not my mother. She was the one who purchased my feminine products every month. One evening, she entered my room in her usual mild-mannered way, informing me that I had a doctor's appointment the next day. As a teen, I was in denial, and my response was a surprise, "For what?" My mother said, "To see how far along you are." I just hung my head down in disbelief, discomfort, and embarrassment. She gave me a loving hug and told me everything would be all right and she would be sure the baby and I would receive proper care. My mother talked to me about prenatal care and vitamins, and I had no clue what she was talking about. I was ignorant of this topic.

The dreaded "next day" arrived. I was anxious. I was nervous. I had butterflies and did not know what to expect. I was a frantic, scared, and lost teenager, but I kept the appointment. The doctor examined me and shared the news. "You are eight weeks pregnant." I heard the doctor's news echo over and over in my head. "How can I break this devastating news to my father?" I wondered. All I could think about was his teenage daughter having a baby out of wedlock and being a disgrace to the family.

After receiving the news, the most challenging part was going back to school. I knew high school would be much different for me. I went from hanging out with friends, clubbing, and going to the skating rink every weekend to dealing with morning sickness, scheduling prenatal visits, and gaining weight. Being a pregnant teenager was a lonely journey. I had no idea I would be separated from my friends and sent to Coronado, a school for pregnant teenagers. As I tip-toed through the hallways from class to class to receive my teacher's signature, I saved my favorite teacher for last. As I approached Ms. CJ's classroom, my stomach felt uneasy. Tears welled in my eyes. As I strolled down the hallway, my pounding heart felt like it was coming out of my chest. I entered the room and handed her my form. She asked, "What is this?" I stood silent as she stood in disbelief; then, she signed in disappointment, grief, and utter shock. I retrieved the form; we locked watery eyes, and I strolled swiftly to the nearest restroom, ran into the stall, slammed the door, and sat there and wept. All I could recall was our many conversations about life decisions and family, and teen pregnancy was not one of them. My only choice at that moment was to start the journey at Coronado.

This was a challenging routine. I got up early to catch the bus to my home school, waited for a different bus to be transported to Coronado, and repeated the same routine after school. I was depleted from catching all the other buses. I would do anything to avoid Ms. CJ when I returned to school in the evening, but she noticed my avoidance and waited for me one day when I exited the bus. Ms. CJ caught me by surprise, but she grabbed my hand and gave me a hug and blessings. That one encounter touched my heart and gave me the courage to get through the pregnancy and make everyone connected to me in any way proud.

On February 19, 1993, I became a mother at eighteen. I had to juggle caring for an infant, sleepless nights, school, work, doctor's appointments, making bottles, and washing extra clothing. I made a grown-up choice as a teenager, unaware of the grown-up responsibilities that came along with that decision. There were days in class I was sleep-deprived because I was up every two hours feeding my lactose-intolerant, colicky, and hungry daughter. She would projectile vomit after her feeds, which meant frequent emergency room and doctor visits for months until the pediatrician finally prescribed a formula she could manage. My daughter's loud cries would not allow me to rest for a few minutes because she was demanding and wanted attention immediately. Most days, I only got three to four hours of uninterrupted rest, yet I managed to get up on time for school every morning, bathe, and dress my baby before leaving the house. As a teenager, I never wanted to be a burden to anyone or put my responsibilities on my family or friends. Still, I depended on my support system to get through this predicament. I was a teenager trying to master motherhood, which resulted in weeping and exhausting nights. Why was I so careless? Why did I become a part of the teen pregnancy epidemic?

I lived with so much anger and bitterness from this crisis, and my negative emotions caused irrational behaviors. If someone said something wrong, I went from calm and collected to uncontrollable rage in minutes. My attitude still did not get in the way of me being a nourishing, giving, and compassionate person. Despite my emotional flaws and the stress of having a daughter, her father and I made it work. He began to work full-time to support us. Years later, he started a flooring business, steadily growing in 2022 despite the pandemic. We were "Bonnie and Clyde!" If he was rocking, I was rolling. What a combination, but we balanced each other.

As a teen mother, I was ridiculed by my peers, frowned upon, judged by adults, and cast aside by church members. It was the whispers I heard that hurt the most. They replayed in my mind. This was a challenging time for my parents, but they never treated me any different or made me feel bad.

What do you do when teachers, church members, associates, and society label you unfit and unsuccessful and expect you to be another teenage dropout with a baby? It went unnoticed that I was educated, successful, and in a stable relationship with the child's father. We worked hard as teenagers to provide for our daughter. We never wanted the label "welfare mom!" I did not live in a home that depended on public assistance, so I wanted the same for my family. Although I was on public assistance for a period, I did not allow that to become my expected end. Public assistance was a steppingstone for our elevation as we made educational decisions to become successful citizens and not become negative labels by society.

I wanted to avoid another pregnancy, so I tried several types of contraceptives; they all made me sick. I planned my life and imagined no more kids until I married. I was not going to disappoint my parents anymore and did not want to be judged by society or receive dirty looks from church folks. I concluded that the best form of birth control was celibacy. However, I did not use that strategy.

There I was again, rehearsing how to tell my parents I was having another baby out of wedlock and thinking about facing the scrutiny of others. Twenty-three months after the birth of my first child, I gave birth to my son on January 20, 1995. I had one child in pull-ups and an infant in pampers. I was back to sleepless nights, making bottles and rewashing extra clothes. I was almost twenty-one years old, repeatedly making grown-folk decisions.

While adding my son to my Medicaid and (SNAP) Supplemental Nutrition Assistance Program benefits, my welfare case worker informed me I could apply for childcare assistance. The state would pay a percentage of the care, and we would pay the remaining portion. I am not proud of relying on the system, but it helped me survive with my first child. I found the best daycare provider in the world, and she was located one street directly behind where I lived at that time. My son loved Ms. G., and she treated him like he was her child. I felt at peace when I had to leave him with her to go to work or class.

I had my routine with my two kids, and things went smoothly for the next four years! Here I go again! The tender breast was the first sign for me with all five pregnancies. Yes, I said five. Morning sickness, fatigue, vomiting, and increased appetite followed. It was time to schedule an OB/GYN appointment. I was no stranger to the gynecologist's office. The doctor ran all the tests and came back with the results. I was four weeks pregnant.

What was I thinking; two miscarriages that my parents had no idea about, two children and now baby #3 at twenty-four years old. In my head, I was telling myself I had to figure out a way to abort this child. I could not keep making false promises to my parents and disappointing them. I could not tell their father because he would be overjoyed. So, I figured I had to do something soon before I got too far along. I called the local abortion clinic every week to receive price quotes for the procedure; the cost would increase every week. I took my kids to school and daycare, worked days, and took classes at night. I felt so dejected at home that I isolated myself from family and close friends. I had daily phone conversations with my friends but avoided in-person visits. Months and months passed, and I was getting bigger and bigger by the day. With this pregnancy, I was enormous and not just my belly. I had swollen legs and feet and had to be evaluated often for toxemia. I purchased extra-large clothing to camouflage my stomach—so I thought.

I came home one evening from class early and tried to run upstairs to my room as I usually did.

My mom knew the routine by now. She was coming out of the kitchen, and my sister was sitting on the couch looking over her eyeglasses. My mother asked for the last time, "When is the baby due?" I responded, "September," as I continued to run up the stairs in sadness, pain, and misery.

On September 24, 1998, baby #3 arrived. This was by far the most complex and painful pregnancy of the three. He weighed 9 pounds and 6 ounces at delivery. I told the doctor after delivery, "Tie my tubes; I do not want any more children." The doctor battled with me. "You might get married one day and want to conceive for your husband." I pleaded with the doctor to please tie my tubes; mission accomplished!

Three successful adults came out of this crisis. I did not see this when I was trying to kill the situation. There were two miscarriages and one cogitated abortion. I had five pregnancies, and all I could see was the pain I caused myself and my parents. Now I feel blessed because the pregnancies were for a purpose. I grew from a frantic, immature, lost teenager to a self-sufficient, educated, and successful mother. It was a painful process, but the suffering was worth it. I am a living testimony that a pregnant teenager can overcome and endure any obstacles!

My crisis EMPOWERED me to see my inner strength and endure as a teenage mother.

Charlene Christian is the mother of two daughters and one grandson. She is a Customer Service Operations supervisor at QVC Inc., where she has been employed for thirty-five years. Charlene is an Intercessor, Intake Staff member, and Bereavement leader at the Mount at Virginia Beach in Virginia. She is a partner with Women Empowered, Inc. She serves as the PR/social media volunteer for Empowerment with Dr. Angie and social media director for the Addicted to Happiness Facebook page. She has graced the runway from Virginia to New York's Fashion on the Hudson as a plus-size model. She had the privilege to walk for Karen Clark Sheard's debut clothing line, Eleven60, and had the opportunity to grace the stage alongside Vicky Winans, Erica Campbell, and Kierra Sheard. While the pulpit is not her platform, she has been licensed to preach the gospel since 2003. She has a prevalent social media presence and often uses the platform to encourage, motivate and inspire her followers. She lives by 2 Corinthians 5:7, "We walk by faith and not by sight."

Connect with Charlene at faithwalkercc@myyahoo.com

CRISIS 12

I Ignored the Signs

Charlene Christian

I still hear the echo of my mother-in-law's voice. She asked, "Did you know he was like that?" Before I could answer, rage rose in my spirit and showed on my face. The nerve of her to ask me if I knew as if I would have responded, "Yes." I also thought, "Is she talking about the guy who would throw his jacket over a puddle of water for me to walk over in the rain?" It certainly could not be. Surely, If I had known, I would not have gone through so much drama or even have married into the mess. Shortly after that conversation with my mother-in-law, my crisis began. I prayed to God to release me from the relationship before I went through the process. I asked, "Why me?" I didn't hear God respond, but I knew He was there to bring me out of what I should have never embraced.

I wondered if I had given him an invitation and permission to abuse me. Was it my fault? Did I deserve it? No! No! No! Who in their right mind gives someone permission to abuse them and stay? Surely not me, but I stayed and hid behind an illusion of an untroubled home. Was there something about me that attracted an abusive man? I did not think so. Was I subconsciously trying to fill a void and embrace trauma I did not need? I did not want to be alone with a newborn baby and felt I needed him. Despite my mother-in-law's speculation, I did not know.

Did I have reservations? Yes, but I did not listen to the voices. When I wanted to get married, I was too nervous to tell my parents face-to-face because I knew it was not right. My dad said, "Do not marry that boy. You and the baby will be fine without marrying him." I knew my dad was not cheering me on and saying it was cool to be a single parent, but wisdom had him suspecting something. I was choosing to get married to do the right thing. I wanted my daughter to be raised in a loving two-parent household.

I pretended the relationship was working when it was not from the beginning. The man had other relationships throughout our ten years of on-and-off dating. Once, he had two of us pregnant at the same time, but he denied my baby right from the start. Unfortunately, I lost my baby, but it was a blessing in disguise.

I was pregnant two years later, and he denied the baby. After I gave birth, he said he did not produce girls because he already had two boys. When my mother-in-law saw our child, she told him he should be ashamed to have said that because the baby was his spitting image.

So, did I have reservations? I sure did, but even after all that, we went through a wedding at the courthouse. When I boldly told my parents we were married, I had the nerve to ask if we could stay with them until we got our place. What foolishness on my part! However, my parents allowed us to stay. It was because of the baby.

What was wrong with my thought process? I have no idea what I was thinking. I guess I did not want to be alone and loved the idea of being married. I later found out my one witness had some reservations as well. She wondered why I was marrying that man. In my clouded mind, I thought we would be together forever. Boy was I in for a rude awakening.

We had been living with my parents for less than a month when he decided to come home at 2:00 in the morning. He was disrespectful, pressing the buttons on the microwave and never hitting start. After a few seconds of hearing the beeps, I went to see if I could help and asked him to come to bed. That is when everything as I knew it changed. He choked me and told me never to tell him what to do. I was shocked, devastated, and heartbroken; however, I remained mute, buttoned up, and close-mouthed.

I vividly remember a moment in the car when he kept turning the radio up loudly to provoke me. I turned the volume down, and he struck me open-handedly on the face with a large ring on his finger. My six-month-old baby was in my arms. I had a black eye and busted and swollen lips. He told me to tell my parents the baby bobbed me in the face with her head. How dare he insert my innocent baby into his heartless actions!

There was even a time when my mom got angry about him mistreating me and slapped him. She was such a rebel! That day, she and I, along with my baby girl, were trampled at the front door as we tried to escape. At that point, I had some questions for God. I needed to know why this was happening and why He was not coming to rescue me. Why had He abandoned me through this crisis? I needed the Lord to do something, but He did not respond.

Not long after the second altercation, he decided to move out and said he would move back with us when I secured our place. At that time, I was so embarrassed because he was leaving the house with no explanation for my parents and left it up to me to explain. It should have ended then, but we signed a lease instead and moved into our own place. I was eager to save our marriage; the abuse continued. The police were called so much that we had to move after only living in the complex for one year. "Why didn't I stop it? I did not know how."

I remember watching my roommate endure abuse, and I vowed never to be in that situation. I had some choice words for my roommate's boyfriend, and I judged my roommate too. I called myself a bad girl trying to rescue my helpless friend from harm. "Who would have guessed I would be next? Not me."

The emotional torment I endured with that man left me confused, anxious, guilty, and ashamed. There were days when the suffering became so unbearable that I just wanted to lie down and die. I thought I was losing it. That is what he was trying to do. He followed me around the house without announcing himself and flicked the lights and TV off and on. I found him lying on the floor beside our daughter's bed. He hid things from me, and I would find them in one of his jacket or pants pockets. He moved the TV remote from my bedside and said I had someone in the house when he was gone. He even took the tire off the car so I could not go anywhere.

Living with him was frightening. I dreaded him coming home at night when intoxicated because it usually meant another verbal attack, another condescending argument, or a drawn-out conversation that led to sex. When he drank, his eyes were piercing, and he turned into a monster, calling me a whore, a bitch, lesbian, gay, and everything else. That was his foreplay. I had to prove to him I was not sleeping with another man—or a woman. I think belittling me and accusing me of being unfaithful hyped him up. Then he manhandled me during sex. I never denied him because he was my husband, and he reminded me of that as often as possible. I would lay there like I was unconscious, so I would not have to feel anything. It was both frustrating and humiliating. It made me sick!

Why didn't I fight back? It was because I knew he could do horrible things to me. I heard about what he had done to women in past relationships, which scared me to death. Some days, I looked at him with disgust and wished he were dead! Yes, I wanted him gone. But at the same time, I still had what I thought was love for him and wanted him to be a father to our daughter. A couple of times while he slept so peacefully, I would get a knife and contemplate slicing and dicing him! If he knew, he would have beat me senseless.

The physical abuse was nothing compared to his emotional and verbal abuse. There was no end to his madness. It is irrational to think I wanted to take the slap or choke over listening to his rude, nasty mouth. In that season of my life, I felt like a strong wind had blown me away, and there was no coming back. My mind was all over the place. One afternoon, my mom asked me to bring her some cookies. I drove to her house and passed the store, never stopping to get the cookies. When I shared with her what happened, she asked, "What is wrong with you?" Are you losing your mind?" I wanted to say, "Yes, Ma, I feel like it." I could never tell her the cause. There were so many sleepless nights when I cried all night long, wondering what I did to make him hate me and what I could do to stop it. I did not feel God anywhere.

The day before Thanksgiving, he picked me up from work. He was intoxicated, and we argued about a gift I received from one of my students. What he said and called me that day broke me down. He accused me of having a lesbian relationship with my best friend. Unbelievable! I was angry and aggravated and did not want to argue, so I threatened to get out of the car. He said, "Get out then!" And I did. This man left me standing on the side of the road in traffic with no way to pick up my baby from my mom's house, who was babysitting, or to get home. He left me! I felt like an idiot.

I began walking across the mall back to my job to make phone calls, but the Lord sent my aunt driving through the parking lot. I got in the car, and, of course, she saw I was upset. She asked what was going on, and I shared my pain with her. She told me I had two choices: stay with him, be quiet, or walk away.

I asked God what to do. He said, "I sent you the answer through your aunt. Did you hear me?" With no hesitation, I pivoted and decided enough was enough, and nothing would change my mind. I had to let him go! I believed that sooner or later, I might end up dead if I stayed. I called the police that night because he would not let me leave. To make me look insane, he came out of the bedroom in his robe, yawning as if he had been in bed the entire night. The police said it was best if one of us left, so I did. The next day, we spoke about my decision, and he tried to talk me out of it, but he reluctantly moved out.

One night some weeks later, he came knocking on the door. To my surprise, I let him in. I noticed right away that he was intoxicated. He refused to leave, saying he was my husband and had the right to be there. I was petrified and began praying like never before that he would get out. He attacked me, and the glass dining table almost fell over me. God answered immediately, and our daughter woke up and ran out to me. He ran to the kitchen, and I took the opportunity to grab her, run to the neighbor's house and knock on the door, even though I knew they were away. He quickly left, and I went back into the house to call 911.

The officers saw the bruises, cuts, and blood coming from my mouth and went to look for him. A brief time later, one officer returned to tell me they found him sitting in the cul de sac and arrested him for domestic assault. The officer added there was no doubt my husband was planning to come back that night and may have killed our child and me. I knew for sure that was it! He harassed me for a while, but soon I heard he had a new fling. Oh, what peace came over me. Unbelievably, we did not divorce until ten years later.

The one thing I would never alter from my experience is giving life to our beautiful daughter, who has brought me so much joy and happiness. I am so grateful to accept the fullness of what was left of the remnants of all the trauma I endured. For a long time, I lived with the guilt of not being a good mother; however, watching her grow up to be a phenomenal woman has exceeded my hopes and dreams, and I am convinced I did well. Had I followed and responded to my initial emotions by aborting our beautiful daughter, I would have deprived myself of experiencing a love like I never knew it before. I know she loves me unconditionally and would do anything possible to ensure I am good.

During the crisis, I wanted to end my life and leave everything behind, but when I thought about my daughter, death was not an option. No matter how I felt, I never said anything against her father because, in time, she would form her own opinion. It is incredible to see today that they have an amazing relationship. I am celebrating because I am still alive and in my right mind. I am grateful for what did not happen. I am truly walking by faith daily.

Although we did not have the best experience in marriage, we shared many unforgettable moments with family and friends. It is essential to know that alcoholism causes the humblest of people to become someone you never knew. I have forgiven him and made peace with myself. There is no more anger dwelling in my heart. The drama could have gone another way, and although I thought I was alone, God was working extremely hard on my behalf. Through it all, He kept me. I stayed for three years, but I finally chose life! Letting go of my past trauma has not been easy because I still have wounds, but I will not allow them to prevent me from fully experiencing my future.

My crisis EMPOWERED me to have a voice for those who endure domestic violence.

Cynthia Wills is the second oldest of four daughters born to Shirley Perry Wills and the late Rev. Joseph Leroy Wills. She has over twenty-five years of Human Services experience in the private, public, and non-profit arenas. She is a Human Services Supervisor with the City of Virginia Beach Department of Human Services in Virginia. Cynthia earned an Associate of Science degree in Clerical Administration from Chowan College, Murfreesboro, NC; a Bachelor of Science degree in Business Administration from Elizabeth City State University, Elizabeth City, NC; a Master of Arts degree in Urban Education (emphasis in Agency Counseling) from Norfolk State University, Norfolk, VA, and a Master of Business Administration degree (emphasis in Human Resource Management) from Strayer University, Virginia Beach, VA. Cynthia has the gift of exhortation to encourage, counsel, and offer sound advice to others as she feels this is the will of God for her life. Cynthia enjoys participating in community service as a proud member of Delta Sigma Theta Sorority, Inc.

Connect with Cynthia at cwills583@gmail.com.

CRISIS 13

I Shall Live and Not Die

Cynthia Wills

—✳—✳—✳—✳—✳—✳—✳—

❝If you do not get any worse, I can save you." Those words, spoken by the hospitalist on January 3, 2021, will be forever etched in my brain and resonate in my spirit. I was not sure whether to cry a sigh of relief or shed tears as I managed to murmur two words just above a whisper, "Thank you." My concern was not whether I would regain full use of my lungs but whether I would be rolled out in a body bag with a tag attached to my toe, Cause of Death: COVID-19.

Deuteronomy 31:6 says, "God will never leave nor forsake you." Yet, I felt I would die a painful death, confined to an impersonal hospital room with no family or friends to render their final goodbyes. With every passing moment, I struggled to breathe and gasp for air; I felt as if I had run a race in the middle of the Arizona sun.

Why God? Why would you allow my family to experience the same agonizing turmoil and emotional heartache that occurred on March 31, 2019, at 4:00 p.m., when our dad died of respiratory failure? Why did it feel like I was operating an old cassette player, rewinding, stopping, and replaying the same dreadful and terrifying scene? It was déjà vu, same hospital, same physicians, and I was questioning God again. "Why would I trust You to save me when You took dad away?" You took away the first man I ever loved, the one who showed me how a real man is to treat a lady and who dedicated his life to your work.

For the second time in three months, dad was admitted for pneumonia. He was first admitted to a hospital in North Carolina on December 20, 2018, while I was admitted to a hospital in Virginia on the same day for a total knee replacement. Unfortunately, the surgery on my right knee resulted in a slow and arduous recovery. Prescription pills did not numb the extreme and excruciating pain, so my physician presented morphine instead, which was administered intravenously; why a morphine drip was not prescribed immediately after surgery is a mystery to me, especially since I suffer from a pain syndrome. Excruciating pain and knee stiffness impaired my ability to achieve an acceptable range of motion. Nevertheless, I was transported to a rehab facility. After the first week's stay, my sister finally told me that my father was in the hospital. Despite their insistence that I stay another week or two, I insisted on being released.

After three months of rehab at my parents' home and not achieving a precise range of motion, I returned to the hospital on March 21, 2019, to have my right knee manipulated. The doctors administered spinal anesthesia and bent the knee to relieve the stiffness and improve the range of motion. Once I was out of recovery, my sister disclosed again that dad had also been admitted to the hospital for a second time the very same day I was admitted. He was being treated for pneumonia. I felt anxious, helpless, and uneasy when I heard the news. Perhaps the uneasiness was caused by my inability to jump in the car and drive from Virginia to North Carolina to check on dad, something I had done numerous times.

Eventually, the awkwardness and restlessness subsided. Self-talk and encouragement became the order of business for the day. I had conversations with God, thanking Him for bringing dad through many dangers seen and unseen, mishaps, health challenges, medical procedures, and too many diagnoses to explain. I was confident dad would survive and thrive as he had done at the rehab facility in December 2018. Sadly, my prayers and pleas were not enough, for God had another plan. The conclusion would be much different and forever change the trajectory of our lives individually and collectively.

While at the hospital, dad was found unresponsive by hospital staff, had to be intubated, and was ultimately admitted to the Intensive Care Unit. During his ten-day hospital stay, things went from bad to worse, with constant moves from a regular room to ICU, to the Stepdown Unit, and back to ICU. The doctors discovered an infection and tumor on his lungs.

As mom engaged in dialogue with family members in the ICU waiting area, one of the nurses, with tears in her eyes, gently shared that he was going into respiratory failure but paid him the best compliment ever. She softly stated, "He's such a nice man." My response to her accolades was to thank her for those kind words: "If you think he's nice in this condition, imagine his thoughtfulness when he's healthy?" I will never forget those words, as they brought me a real sense of peace.

How would I tell mom the news that her soulmate of sixty years was slowly dying? We gathered in dad's room to say our goodbyes. As his four daughters, two sons-in-law, adult grandchildren, two nieces, and an uncle who had driven from New York and other relatives entered the room, we shared our love for him and how much his love had meant to us over the years. As much as I wanted God to keep him among us, his breathing was becoming shallower. Softly, I whispered in his ear. "Take your rest, dad. You do not have to hold on to another moment. I promise to take care of mom in your absence."

As it was too traumatic and challenging to witness his struggling to inhale and exhale, I quickly switched from daughter mode to social worker mode. I dried and wiped the tears from my eyes, held my head high, and walked outside the ICU room to find the ICU nurse. Most compassionately and sympathetically, I asked if he was in pain or suffering and if she could give him something to make him comfortable as we removed the oxygen mask and disconnected the machine pumping air into his lungs. For my sanity, I had to remain in social worker mode. Otherwise, I would have crawled into his hospital bed, laid my head on his chest, and begged God not to take him away. Yet, I knew he was tired and had labored in the vineyard long enough.

The previous night, the hospitalist took the liberty to explain dad's condition and provided mom and me with only two medical options available to dad. In the middle of the explanation, dad motioned for me to lift the oxygen mask as he wanted to speak. In typical dad fashion, he raised his pointer finger, gazed at me, and clearly said without struggling, "Do what the majority say do because I am ready to go home." Thank God mom did not overhear what he had just said.

Years prior, dad told my mom and me that he never wanted to be kept alive by artificial measures. We honored his wishes and requested that he be removed from life support. We said our goodbyes as he took his last breath on Sunday, March 31, 2019, just two days after he and mom celebrated their 60th wedding anniversary. His death certificate would read like a medical diary – respiratory failure (ten days), pneumonia (seven days), and septic shock listed as a contributing factor.

Now you can understand how conflicted I felt about going to this place of gloom and doom. Was I to stay home and fight COVID-19 alone or muster up enough energy to drive myself to this God-forsaken hospital referenced as "the morgue?" I chose to do the latter. As I stood up at home to walk to the shower, the room began to spin as if I had been hypnotized, and I started panting for air. I thought if I could shower, I would feel a sense of triumph and accomplishment. I finally showered. As I stepped out, my energy level rapidly declined. My body began shutting down as I laid across the bed and experienced uncontrollable diarrhea. My bodily functions were doing their own thing. I unwrapped the towel from my body and placed it between myself and the bed. What a horrible feeling! I felt like someone who had just eaten green beans, sweet potatoes, and corn mixed with a hint of Ex-Lax. I returned to the shower a second time and, afterward, managed to remove everything from the bed, threw it in the washer, sprayed the home with Lysol, dressed, and drove myself to the same hospital where we witnessed dad on his death bed.

As I inappropriately parked in the handicapped space, I got out and found myself stopping every few steps to gasp for air. It seemed like it took an eternity to walk from the handicapped section of the parking lot to the emergency room. Once inside, a young female employee asked if I was experiencing breathing problems. As I nodded, I could feel tears welling in my eyes and falling down my cheeks. Rather than testing my oxygen level, she placed me in a wheelchair, where I waited for about an hour and a half. Once seen, the triage nurse noticed I was in distress and asked if I was having trouble breathing. When I stated yes, she quickly called an ER nurse who tested my oxygen level using an oximeter and immediately placed me on oxygen. Again, that ticker tape began scrolling in my head of dad's death.

God, how did I get to this point? How did I go from being a joyous, fun- loving, living, breathing human being to having an oxygen tube attached to both nostrils all day, hauling around an oxygen tank? I was uncertain of whose report to believe. Would I trust God's report, which says, "He who breathed life into my lungs will keep me safe from harm?" I trusted Him to save my dad, the Patriarch, and the glue that kept our family together. Yet, because of his death, everyone was impacted emotionally, spiritually, and mentally. Even my great-niece, six years old at the time, cried when she learned of my dad's passing. She described him as "such a funny great-granddaddy." When she asked her father if her great-granddaddy had died, her father offered a compassionate response. "Yes, great-granddaddy passed away and is now in heaven." She struggled to comprehend and process what she had just learned. Filled with love, heartbreak, and disappointment, she wiped away tears as she said, "But I prayed for him." Despite her prayers, she did not understand why her great-granddaddy would be taken away in her six-year-old mind.

I did not understand either. What God allowed to happen took an emotional toll on the family.

How could I trust God to save me during this near-death experience? Before being admitted, I had experienced every symptom except a fever, including excruciating headaches, loss of taste and smell, extreme tiredness, body aches, nausea, and difficulty breathing because pneumonia covered 80% of my lungs. My circumstances felt overwhelming and insurmountable. The emotional turmoil and stress of being in the same hospital that took our dad away were too much to handle. As I lay in that uncomfortable hospital bed and pondered what was happening around me, I received the investigational drug Remdesivir for pneumonia; Vitamins C, D, and Zinc to build the immune system; antibiotics; and steroids to combat infection. I was discharged with an oxygen tank for three months to be used around the clock. Soon I could finally see the light as my condition improved.

Because of my crisis, I have become a more empathic person. The storm sent to break and kill me proved to be the storm God used to make me. My predicament empowered me to love, cherish, and appreciate family and friends while I can because tomorrow is never promised.

**My crisis EMPOWERED me to
become more empathic.**

Dewanna Seward is the founder, visionary, and CEO of Indoor/Outdoor Reach LLC, an organization for youth where their wounds are healed from the inside out. She is also the CEO of Lil Angel's Styles, focusing on unique hairstyles for youth. Her motto, "Our Youth is Our Future," embodies a second chance for any decision when the effort is put into changing. A native of Portsmouth, VA, and graduate of Virginia State University in Petersburg, VA, Dewanna's passion is to save youth from tragic situations and heal their parents. In the future, she plans to open a youth center for troubled teens where their mental health is addressed, and parents can be redirected to change the trajectory of their lives. She draws strength for this journey from the loss of her son, Jhenesis D'mor, whose legacy she keeps alive for others by sharing, "Just Don't Lose Faith."

Connect with Dewanna at www.jdcreationss.com

CRISIS 14

Do Not Give Up

Dewanna Seward

As a little girl, I was lost. Anger, betrayal, abandonment, and other emotions gripped my life, and I did not know how to cope. Recently, I finally learned to express and release my feelings as I sought healing and committed myself to growing through my pain.

My crisis drew me to Spider-Man. I saw myself in him and my tangled life in his webs. Each web represents trauma I have overcome. Spider-Man spends his time-saving people, fighting to prove who he is, and trying to conquer the world. He does it all while hiding his identity because he fears judgment. He knows how to put his mask on and fight each battle with all his might. He is my inspiration because I was afraid of judgment for so long. I just wanted to be accepted, so I thought I could save the world, and I fought all my battles (trauma and emotions) with every ounce of fight in me.

My mother was a young mother that decided to move from our hometown in North Carolina when I was a baby. Her career path and a relationship at the time led her to come to Virginia. When she relocated to Virginia, she became pregnant with my little brother. However, my mother worked many hours to provide for us. Her providing for us left us with my little brother's family, which I did not find out who they were until I was older. So, while with them, there was an aunt that I clung to and loved being around. My aunt, her boyfriend, and I spent every day with one another except when they were at work. I was hurt when she went to college, but she came home for her birthday, and I was excited. However, she went to the store and got hit by a drunk driver, and the family hid it from me for a while. When my aunt died, I felt abandoned because I did not know where she was, and at the time, I did not think anyone loved me as she did.

As we got older, we spent more time at our grandmother's house when my mother would work out of town or long hours a day. While staying with my brother's family, when I was about seven, I discovered that we had separate families, and it began to start feeling like it. I was always blamed for everything; I got in trouble for every little thing, and no one listened. Several of us stayed in this house, and I was the only girl child, but the children had to stay in a room and watch tv unless we were eating. A great-uncle came home from jail and stayed, sexually abusing me or touching me inappropriately as a child. I could not tell anyone because he threatened me, and I was always called a liar, no matter what I said. Then, I had to watch my brother and cousin "fondle" themselves." They played with their private parts, watched porn, and asked me to touch them and allow them to feel me.

Unless we went to the bathroom or ate dinner, we had to stay in the bedroom. When I tried to escape, I would get fussed at by a family member. My mother worked so much that she made sure all our time was occupied so that we would not notice she was not around as much. Her tactic did not work because I acted out in every way possible. My only excitement came during the summer when we went to my grandmother's house. She allowed us to be children, spend time with family, attend Vacation Bible School, enjoy trips, and attend family reunions. However, the sexual abuse did not stop. My mother's two brothers were the perpetrators. Other adults claimed they were "off" and did not know any better. One uncle was in a wheelchair, and the other one had mental disabilities.

As I reflect on my experiences, I see myself as Spidey, fighting through webs to become the empowered woman I am today. One of the first webs I conquered was trying to fit in. Because I was sexually abused and looked at as a sex object, I assumed it was fine for others to treat me that way. My mom stopped traveling for work when my behavior got out of control. That gave me more time to be a child. I had been a sex object for so long that I became accustomed to sexual comments and advances. It did not pair well with my low self-esteem. I did not have many friends. The few friends that I had took advantage of my kindness.

I played basketball growing up, but the connection always seemed off for me. In middle school, we had to move due to the neighborhood being torn down. Now we are in a new area, where I chose to hang out with gang members or boys. You could not tell me I was not a part of the gang or one of the guys. I was willing to do whatever they asked me to do, so I fought hard to fit in. Later, it cost me my body. We would stay out and smoke, but everything turned out worse for me when we walked back to the neighborhood or our courts. The guys would beg me to suck their private parts and threaten to kick me out of the group if I did not. Because I wanted to be accepted by the guys, I did what they asked. I would say, "Why not? I was used to being sexually abused by some of my family anyway."

Trying to fit in also made me feel unprotected and unloved. When I went home crying, I was not comforted. Instead, my mother met me with anger. She called me disrespectful and antagonistic things but never once asked why I was late, where I had been, or if I was ok. I was not heard, and she did not care. It was hurtful, so I stayed out later and acted out more. I was tired of hearing, "The way your attitude is, you are going to end up dead or in jail. You are so fast in the ass, you will be pregnant or in jail soon."

One day, my mother locked me out of the house. I got upset when she forced me to do something, so she kept saying, "Stay out there. You want to be grown." When I broke my bedroom window to get into the house, she called my dad to pick me up, which was my wish. My father finally showed up the next day, and I went to Alabama with him. My mother did not allow me to take any of my things which was fine. I was excited to be with my father but that move was like swinging into another tangled web. We took our time on our trip down South, and I also got to see my sister. I did not know my sister or have a bond with her. At first, nothing bothered me until I found out my father was homeless. I was fine staying in a car, hopping from one woman's house to the next, watching my father drink day in and day out, and seeing my father do drug transactions. I was too young or lost to know what was going on. He applied for several apartments, and a month later, when we finally got approved, we had to wait two weeks for the move-in date.

After a while, I got tired of watching him do the same boring routine, so I just stayed with my older cousin until we moved into our own apartment. While staying with her, we got high off marijuana, and I did what I wanted. I felt like a grownup. Smoking kept me calm and suppressed my emotions, but I was not old enough to use such a reckless coping mechanism. After two weeks of this fun, my dad and I moved into the apartment, established rules, and set a daily routine.

One day, I was so excited to meet him at home after his day at work and my day at school. For the first time, I was going to show my father my report card, and I was excited about it. My excitement went out the window once I unlocked the door, only to have it slammed in my face. He was in the apartment with several women having sex. I waited, thinking that the door would open soon. When it did not, I wrote him a letter informing him of all the webs that caused me to be the way I am. I left it on the porch and walked down the sidewalk to my aunt's apartment. While I waited there for him, my excitement turned into anger and rage. Once again, I felt abandoned.

It was dark, after 11:00 p.m., when my father came to my aunt's apartment to get me. I was hurt; my father was the only person I depended on for love, and he turned his back on me. It was not my fault that I stayed out late that night; he was the one who slammed the door in my face. I had no choice except to go to my aunt's apartment. He was so upset and made the decision that I had to permanently leave Alabama. He dropped his fourteen-year-old daughter off at the bus station in the middle of the night. I had to figure out the rest on my own. He drove me from Alabama to the bus station in Atlanta so that I could catch the next bus to Virginia. I sat at the station for hours. I finally made the dreaded call to my mother. At first, she was concerned, but then she fussed without asking my side of the story; I hung up on her. I called my girlfriend and explained the situation to her at that moment. She talked with her mom, who purchased a ticket for me to go to her house in Maryland. I did not want to be around my family anymore.

I was webbing, swinging, fighting through life, and trying to rebuild myself. My girlfriend›s family welcomed me and loved me in a way that was new to me. Their home was filled with love, and they communicated openly, even in heated situations. They did things as a family, too. While learning to communicate, I told my mother about my sexuality and how I was uncomfortable with the clothes she sent me. Her reply was the most hurtful thing. "I didn't raise you like that," she said. Then she hung up on me. We did not have contact with each other for some time. Once again, I was abandoned.

As I tried to heal, the perfect family kicked me out. My girlfriend could not tolerate my mood swings and did not want to be with me anymore. I felt abandoned, heartbroken, betrayed, and alone because I could not call my family. My brother's family had turned against me because I was too bad, and they disapproved of my sexuality. My grandmother did not want to deal with my attitude, and my parents abandoned me at that point. I was battling depression, abandonment, and suicidal thoughts, so I took things into my own hands. I ended up staying with a friend, working, and finishing eleventh grade.

During that time, I became a very wild child. I tried to control my emotions by smoking and drinking every day. Yes, there was an adult in the home, but we did what we wanted. It did not dawn on me to slow down until my mother's job called, saying my mother was in the hospital. She called me from the hospital and said, "I love you no matter what. You are my baby." I cried and went home to Virginia that weekend. My mom was released from the hospital, but she was still struggling. She was living with one of my childhood friends from the projects who had just had a baby—my godson. Although I was concerned about them, I did not like the dysfunction or separation, so I returned to Maryland. When I arrived, I was more determined to work harder to save money, finish school, and get back home to help my mother.

My last and most decisive web propelled me to a better future. Seeing my godson inspired me. I was tired of ‹wilding› out. After finishing school, my mother traveled to Maryland to pick me up. My godson and I were inseparable. He was the push I needed to better myself. When I enrolled in school, all my credits did not transfer, so they tried to tell me I could not graduate. When people did not believe I could do something, I was motivated to prove them wrong. I finished my senior year by completing two-night classes each semester which kept me in school from six in the morning until ten at night. I was the DECA president, maintained the honor roll all year, and stayed out of trouble even though I was labeled a troublemaker before I left. After high school, I was accepted to Virginia State University.

As Spidey, I swung, webbed, fought, and conquered every crisis that came my way. I wanted to be different, so I pushed myself. I was raised in the church and believed in prayer, but I always questioned why I had to go through so much at an early age. I often kept fighting to prove I was more significant than my circumstances. I would recite Philippians 4:13, "I can do all things through Christ who strengthens me."

Some relatives still would not listen to me, accept what they did not see happen to me, or try to understand that I acted out for attention. However, the attention they continuously wanted to show me was taking me to doctors, making me take medicine, and silencing my voice from the doctors, psychiatrists, and family. It did not work. I continued to fight for freedom in my crisis. My healing did not begin until my son, Jhenesis D'mor, was born. When I first laid eyes on him, I could only smile. I vowed that I would not take him through what I went through. His life would be different. Unfortunately, he was only with us for eighty-three days. He succumbed to SIDS, Sudden Infant Death Syndrome. I was hurt but, I experienced my dream become a reality and nightmare all at the same time. Today, I am grateful I cherished him with everything in me during his short time here and even now. When he went to be with the Lord, I was grateful for what God had done because I was so focused on my son that I had stopped focusing on my healing from all the trauma I had endured as a teenager. I thought I was healed, but I realize I just swept things under the rug.

Everyone I once broke my neck for was invisible when my baby died. This was like abandonment all over again, but I learned how to cope with it during counseling. I also learned to say "NO" and obey God's voice instead of mine. I pray more than I talk to others, and I enjoy talking to my counselor weekly for insight about releasing this generational curse of abandonment. I now realize I did not have to continue to live with it as part of my life.

My crisis EMPOWERED me to overcome abandonment.

Vanessa Vaughan is a native of Portsmouth, Virginia. She is the mother of five children and five grandchildren. Because of her love for serving others, she has been in nursing for over thirteen years. Both youth groups and social services have recognized her for her achievements in this profession and childcare. She is known for her passion for helping children. She has demonstrated this by opening her home to her nieces and nephews and young boys and girls to nurture and care for them with the love of Christ. She is the founder of Touched by an Angel Ministry and the Proprietor of Kreative Anointing Hands. In this business, she creates beautiful memories through books and photo albums of special occasions for people to cherish.

Vanessa is also passionate about authoring books where she believes God's grace has allowed her to overcome her trials and tribulations through his love.

Connect with Vanessa at vanessavaughan1121@gmail..com

CRISIS 15

Abducted in Plain Sight

Vanessa Vaughan

—✷—✷—✷—✷—✷—✷—✷—

Silently crying inside myself while trying to hold back emotions of bitterness, shame, anger, and embarrassment, my past became my present situation. What happened next took me by surprise. When I realized it was not a bad dream, I panicked in fear as I relived my childhood abduction. The cold feeling of sweat and tears dripped down my face while I was exhaling and trying to catch my breath. As every moment from that dark place, the day of my trauma, came rushing through my mind, the haunting flashbacks had already begun to unfold. I wanted it all to go away, but it did not. As the tears started to flow faster, I screamed, "God, why did you reveal his face?" This crisis was something I fought hard not to remember for years. God then spoke, "It's for my glory."

It was an ordinary day when my mom sent me to the store. My best friend, Micah, came along with me. As we were walking, out of nowhere, an older model, brown and beige car, pulled beside us and stopped. An unfamiliar man driving said, "I am looking for your mother's house, Alpine." With no forethought of being in danger, I looked at my friend and asked her to ride with me to show him where my mother lived. She refused, stood outside the car when I got in, then turned as if she was headed back toward my house. Before she left, I asked her to tell my mother that I would show her friend where we lived. She departed, and the man pulled off with me in the car. "Why did I get into the car with an unfamiliar man?" Because he called my mother's name, I felt no reason to fear him. At the age of thirteen, I assumed that he knew my mother and that he was her friend.

The car pulled off, and it was not until I pointed in the direction for him to turn that I knew I was in trouble because he kept straight. I panicked, cried, and pleaded with him to let me out. He refused, locked the car door, and said, "If you touch the locks, I will cut you." As he said this, I saw the silver, sharp blade of the knife coming towards me. My emotions were scattered; I was terrified because I did not know what would be next. He continued to drive out of our complex, and then he looked at me as he was driving and told me to come closer. I had no choice but to obey him because he still had the knife in his hand. Driving slowly, he put the knife down and then unbuttoned my shorts. I begged again, "Please take me home." So many things were going through my mind, and I began to shake and cry, not knowing how to respond to this crisis at the age of thirteen. After unbuttoning my shorts, he slowly put his hands in my panties and fondled my vagina.

I was in shock and could not move. The trauma was horrifying. It upset my stomach; I wanted to vomit. I had to hold back the throw-up in the back of my throat. Afraid he might cut me as he sexually assaulted me in ways pleasing to him, but agonizing to me, I kept quiet. I was confused and in mental and physical pain as he smelled his fingers and looked at me, saying, "You smell good." I know now, during that dreadful moment which seemed like hours, I was being violated; my innocence was stolen by someone I thought was my mother's friend. At that time, all I could think as a young girl was, "Will I ever be able to live a normal life after this crisis?"

Well, the crisis did not end there. We finally came to a complete stop in a parking lot that was familiar to me. I had been here before because my dad worked at the Shipyard. He instructed me to get on his lap while we were still in the car. Again, I had no choice except to obey. He said, "Don't yell; don't scream, or I will hurt you." He sexually assaulted me while I was on his lap. Still in shock and emotionally drained, I could not speak, and I had no more tears to cry; I was numb. I was helpless, and he was in complete control. I thought, "How could a grown man hurt a child this way?" I had no answer. During this time, I knew I would be rescued when the car was parked because I saw people walking to their vehicles. My head was peering over the steering wheel, and I could see through the front of the windshield while I sat on my abductor's lap. No one saw me in plain sight. But there was my help! As he took advantage of this thirteen-year-old girl, I looked away to distract myself from the pain he was inflicting upon me; when I turned my head, I saw a Bible lying in the middle of the back seat. I immediately stopped crying when I saw the Bible, and a calmness overwhelmed me. I suddenly turned my head toward him and said, "If you take me home, God will forgive you." Once I made that statement, the molestation stopped! I was shocked that what I said caused him to stop! The nightmare had come to an end. I could not understand; I had been begging him to take me home the entire day, but he refused, threatened, and ignored me. The whole time I was in the car, I pleaded with him to take me home. It was not until I spoke the words, "God will forgive you if you take me home," that he listened.

He drove me back and dropped me off where I was abducted. His last words to me, and I will never forget, "If you tell anybody, I will come back to hurt you." I got out of the car in a daze, confused, overwhelmed, and afraid to go home. I was so traumatized that I sat under a nearby tree to get myself together. His car was pulling off, and I looked to get the license plate numbers. I could only see three because I was so distraught, my vision was blurred, and I was in physical pain. I sat there in distress. I brought my knees up, wrapped my arms around them, and bowed in defeat. I felt unclean! "How can I go home and live a child's life as I once did?" Confused, I became frustrated and said, "I couldn't!" There was no way I could have my childhood life back after this predator violated me. Not only was this haunting me, but how would I face my mother and tell her of this dreadful ordeal? Again, thoughts of fear flooded my mind, and the conclusion came to me, "I was going to be beaten by my mother." She would not understand, especially if Micah had not given her my message.

I did not remember the walk home; however, it seemed forever for a short distance, five minutes. I was hoping not to run into any of my friends, especially Micah. I felt embarrassed and ashamed, and I wanted to go home and take a bath. When I finally reached my house, I felt relief. I walked up the steps, and there she was, opening the screen door. She had a stern look on her face as if she were angry. She raised her voice and asked, "Where the hell have you been?" I quickly slid pass her in the house, and I proceeded to explain what had happened. My voice is shivering, "Someone took me in their car and would not bring me home." Without telling the entire story, leaving out how I was molested, she smacked me in my face with her open hand. I became angry because I was looking for comfort from my mother; instead, she added to the trauma. I wanted her to hug me and tell me everything would be fine. I just wanted a "mother's love." The good thing she did was call the police and report the kidnapping. As we were waiting for them, there was not a quiet moment. All I could hear was my mother fussing about me getting in my abductor's vehicle. It was too much to deal with. So, I blocked out the yelling and put up an invisible wall. My mother continued to stand at the door, yelling while the police arrived. She directed me to go outside, and she followed me. I obeyed, and they took my statement and then showed me a book with pictures of men who had abducted children. As the officer flipped each page, the faces of the men were blurred. No one looked familiar; I had already begun to shut down and did not want to remember. The trauma had already started to take effect. The police officer looked at my face and noticed my pain. He closed the book and said, "You're one of the lucky ones who made it home."

Was I lucky? I would not call it luck; I would call it "purpose in my abduction." Purpose because I now know what it is God has called me to do. God allowed me to survive my evil abductor. This scripture I have lived since that time, "You planned evil against me; God planned it for good to bring about the present result – the survival of many people. I am a survivor" (Genesis 50:20, CSB). I am not saying God planned the crisis, but what He did was turn it for my good. I am living today for the many young girls still struggling with molestation and sharing their testimony. I could not break free alone. I needed help.

First, I surrendered to God. This meant putting my complete trust in Him and leaning not to my understanding. In doing this, I submitted my heart, mind, and soul to the one who could fix my situation. When I fully surrendered and submitted to God, I saw Him order my steps to the next phase of my healing which was Christian counseling. When I began my counseling sessions, I had numerous breakthroughs and was no longer bound. To be free, I had to tell my dreaded story. I had to face the dark places of every moment when I was violated, molested, and fondled. I had to describe how my life was threatened at thirteen and how I felt I would never live to tell how I made it out alive. Finally, I had to have Faith in God in the process. I needed to allow God to take complete control of my steps. When I was ready, after surrendering, submitting, and going to counseling, He had prepared me for my purpose. I was ready to move forward, but I needed to forgive.

One day, God directed me back to the church of my childhood and adult years; when I left I was shattered. I got out of the car and slowly walked to the church's door. Standing by the door, I said, "I forgive you." After making that verbal declaration, I looked up as the sun beamed on my face, and there was a beautiful cross atop the church. In all the years I attended, I had not seen the cross until that day. It was a sign from God because there was a peace that overwhelmed me, symbolizing my FREEDOM!

I am free! I can truly walk in my healing and purpose to be an effective witness to the world. Nothing, not even my crisis, can separate me from the love of God. During and after this ordeal, I wanted to curse my situation and God because I felt alone. It was not until I saw God show up, the Bible on the back seat of the car, that I realized God was there. I know

He was there because He brought me out, and I am telling my story. This ordeal gave me a purpose. I have a voice to be the catalyst to help other young girls to come out of hiding and tell their stories because telling is a significant part of the healing process.

My crisis EMPOWERED me to be a healing voice to the molested.

EMPOWERED to...

The outcome of the crisis in each narrative has given you hope. I am sure you saw yourself in one of these stories. Whether it was domestic violence, physical and emotional abuse, divorce, single teenage mother, molestation, rejection, financial difficulty, abandonment, or grief, you related to one or more of these experiences. The question is, "What does it EMPOWER you to?"

There is always a reason we experience a crisis; however, we tend to want to know why instead of seeking revelation while we are in it. Each of us has released our inner emotions during our crises and how they changed the trajectory of our destinies. If we had not stayed in the process until the end, we would have never been empowered to become who it is we are today. You heard us echoing the pain and rejection from the crises, but they did not have power over us. They did not destroy us; they did not derail us, nor did they deter us. What did our crises do? They EMPOWERED us to be better than our crises and share our stories.

Through your crisis, what are you empowered to do, or whom are you empowered to become? It is a question only you can answer, but you must go through the process of the crisis to the end! It is only then that you are EMPOWERED to your NEXT!

Made in the USA
Middletown, DE
16 February 2023

24774624R00130